The Real Livingston
– A Kaleidoscope

Written and compiled by

Ian Colquhoun – 2013

Acknowledgments

Big thanks to the following people for their contributions, help and support, one way or another, in the journey that has been writing this book.

My family, my friends, Cybil Cavanagh, Emma Peattie and the other kind people at West Lothian Archives, Tom Kerr, West Lothian Council, Debbie Hall and the 'Courier, Peter Johnston, Angela Constance, Graeme Morrice , The McDermott family, Ewen Gallacher, Nicci MacKerracher, The guys at Livingstoni, Sandra Dick, West Lothian Writers' Forum, Craigshill Library, David Cicero, Eddie Anderson, Alex Stewart, Mary Gapinski, Elizabeth Ferguson, The Livingston Inn, Alec Muir, Brendan Moohan, Brian Cullion, Mary Gapinski, Mark Strachan, Craig Smith, Sean and Paul O'Donnell, Craig Smith, Susan Docherty, Sandra Lawton, Joe McDermott, Stuart Pearson, Kenny Omond, Keith Tait, The McGregor family, and anybody else I've forgotten to mention.

ISBN: 978-1-291-49498-3

www.publishnation.co.uk

This book is dedicated to the memory of the late Robin Cook MP, may he rest in peace, and also dedicated to my teacher from Primary 7 at Letham, Miss Morrison, for seeing my talent, rather than my attitude.

I'd also like to thank and offer my love and best wishes to everybody from Livingston, young and old, from school, work or play, that I grew up with, whether we got on or not – we've all been part of each other's lives. God bless you all. Ian.

Foreword from Angela Constance MSP

My most enjoyable flights into Edinburgh Airport are when the plane flies over Livingston. You get a great overview of the size and shape of the town with its many recognisable landmarks and easily identifiable communities. When viewing Livingston from above, you can really see the logic of the town planners as well as the structure and the simplicity of 'the plan'. But this book, written and compiled by Ian Colquhoun, is so not about town planning, instead it's a social history and therefore wonderfully compliments and contrasts with existing works on Livingston.

In essence, 'The Real Livingston – A Kaleidoscope' is a collection of snapshots about life in Livingston, across the centuries but mostly about the contemporary and most importantly, it's about people. It won't be everybody's cup of tea, but actually that's what I really like about it, it is rather raw in parts - it's real.

There are parts of this book that I could really connect with; the account from O'Driscoll about his long years of service as a youth worker brought back many memories of my own career in social work, and who could fail to be touched by the tribute to Kerry McGregor, and at last finding out who Lizzie Bryce really was! There are also some wonderful little oddities and surprises such as the streaker in the Livingston Inn and even the activities of the body snatchers in 1823. I can assure you there is something in this book for every Livingstonian.

The kaleidoscope approach works really well, enabling you to dip in and out, but the book is given an overall coherence by the two bookends. The first bookend is the introduction by the author and the second bookend is the collection of very personal accounts by a diversity of town residents, and their perspective of life in Livingston. From my reading there is one big theme, like a thread running throughout the book - and that's jobs. Over the course of decades, 'The Real Livingston – A Kaleidoscope' charts the highs and lows of job creation and job losses.

Part and parcel of the hopes and dreams of the new town was a new life with a new house and a job. The introduction rightly highlights the need for sustainable employment past and present. Inward investment was and is important to Livingston and to Scotland, but there is a lament throughout the book that craves economic diversity, questions why we put all our eggs in one basket and voices a desire for more indigenous home grown business that creates a more stable environment for sustainable employment.

Given the recent death of Baroness Thatcher there is a very topical assessment of 'Thatcherism' and the devastation it caused to West Lothian. It was growing up in Thatcher's Britain that made this West Lothian lass a Scottish Nationalist. Having seen first-hand the impact of unemployment on my own family and community in the 1980s, it's quite poignant for me now to be the Scottish Government Minister for Youth Employment. Tackling all forms of unemployment and underemployment is not just a political crusade - it has to be a personal commitment.

Of course there are many parallels with today and the 1980s, for example, we have another Tory Government that West Lothian and Scotland most certainly did not vote for. I just want Scotland to get the Government it votes for, not just some of the time but each and every time. But I am just one voice with one vote. Livingston folk, like others will have to make up their own mind in September 2014.

I have had the privilege of representing Livingston either as a local Councillor or as a Parliamentarian for 16 years and I have always been struck by the strong sense of community and identity. I used to think of Livingston as a collection of villages, but in addition to the distinct communities of Craigshill, Ladywell, Howden, Carmondean, Dedridge, Knightsridge, the Village, Deans and Murieston, there is now, most definitely, a solid Livingston identity.

An identity forged by, amongst other things, shops, football, a hospital but most of all an identity forged by people. All people and all communities have frailties but they also have strengths and Livingston's great asset is its people. There are many unsung heroes in Livingston, a bit like the youth worker and others featured in this book, who for precious little reward or recognition have tirelessly given their time, energy and sometimes their money to make Livingston a better place.

This book very much captures the life in Livi - the good and the bad, the strengths and the weaknesses, the deficits as well as the assets, but most of all it's a book about people, the people of Livingston.

ABOUT THE AUTHOR AND THIS BOOK

I was born 400 years ago in the highlands of Scotland. I am immortal, and I am not alone. Now is the time of the gathering, when the stroke of a sword will unleash…no wait a minute, that's the plot of 'Highlander'. I'll try again.

Most authors write this part of their book in the third-person perspective, but I won't. I was born at Bangour in 1978 and grew up in Craigshill, where I was educated at Letham Primary School, then Craigshill High School and subsequently at Inveralmond, after Craigshill High closed. I liked the first two schools but hated Inveralmond, probably because the disruption of moving there came at a time when there was already great disruption of another kind in my life, and also because Inveralmond was a failing school at the time. I left school after missing a lot of 4th year because of illness, and got a job in a local warehouse. I worked in three different warehouses in West Lothian until I was twenty-four, then I moved to Ireland. My own personal Livingston story is much like many others'. As a boy I loved playing football in Craigshill, particularly during the summer holidays. Games would start at ten in the morning, with maybe four or five of us. By lunchtime there'd be ten of us. By afternoon we could be up to about fifteen-a-side. Then most would disappear to get their dinner, then we'd play football until it got dark, different people coming and going from the game throughout the day. Those gargantuan, long summer days in Craigshill playing football are the happiest memories of the town that I retain, asides those of a few special women and some great nights clubbing with friends.

I also went to Youth Theatre for a while and went swimming a lot as a boy. When I hit my mid-teens football took over my life in a different way, as I followed Hibs, never missing a home game and attending games with various people from Livingston and Edinburgh. My 'hobby' for years was getting drunk and watching Hibs, singing our songs with my mates and taunting opposing fans. As a result of this I ended up spending a lot of time in Edinburgh as a teenager, which was cool as , asides from work, there wasn't much to do in Livingston back then, until you were old enough to get served in pubs.

I never missed Livingston at all when I left in 2002, but I do miss a lot of its people, nevertheless, I will always see the town as 'home'.

As for this book, it was a real journey to write, and a thoroughly enjoyable journey at that. I had to omit a lot of things I found in the archives because they concerned people that I know, or have known. Where possible I have tried to minimise the number of entries about violent crime, but you'll find that almost every entry in the 'On this Day' section is a story that concerns Livingston life and Livingston's people – all other previous books about the town, though great books, have been focused on town planning, LDC and photos – with no 'real' stories in them. The kaleidoscope effect of the 'On this Day' section, and the written contributions I have included from others after it, will hopefully give the reader a glimpse of the *real* Livingston. This is not a book containing all of 'Livingston's pivotal events', as such a book would be about eight-feet thick and weigh more than an elephant with a fridge strapped to its back, but I hope that you enjoy it nonetheless. I'm about to release an 'On this Day' book about Edinburgh, but as I am a Livingston lad, I found writing this book more enjoyable. I included contributions from others because a simple myopic book just by me wouldn't tell the whole story at all. I, and my contributors, have by no means written the full story either, but working together, we've made the best attempt at it so far. I hope that one day, a better author than I will write an even bigger, better one, and I look forward to reading it.

I myself wrote the opening chapter and the entire 'On this Day' section, my contributors' pieces are individually credited. Special thanks to the guys at the Livingstoni website for letting me use some of their photos.

All exact dates were obtained from West Lothian Archives, Linlithgow Local History Centre, the archives of The Livingston Post and the West Lothian Courier, national newspaper archives, Edinburgh Central Library George IV Bridge, the book 'Livingston Lives' by Emma Peattie, the book 'The history of Livingston' by William F Hendrie, and from a good few learned friends and sources in Livingston.

Livingston: A Reflection

The creation of Livingston, and of all the other 'New-Towns' was arguably the biggest social-engineering project undertaken in the British Isles since the Plantation of Ulster in the early 17th century, certainly since the Industrial Revolution at least. On simple analysis the creation of Livingston was in many ways a quite ridiculous idea, in some respects. Think about it at face-value for a moment. Someone in an office in London decided to build a town in the middle of nowhere, amid a cluster of old mining villages that had been in steady economic decline for decades. The people who were to come and inhabit this New-Town were expected to be from outwith the general area, meaning that most of the families and individuals would potentially be leaving behind not only the towns and cities that they called home, but also the 'safety net' that many people had through their extended families, which at the time was greatly important to many people. Then there were of course, the economic issues, number one being first, foremost and always, jobs/employment.

Of course, the flip-side of those considerations makes the idea of moving to such a new town an attractive proposition. A fresh start. New, better housing. Safer streets for children to play in. New opportunities in new industries and new job opportunities, less pollution, and of course, the chance to be part of a revolutionary social-experiment. The biggest question that many people will ask of the new-towns, and certainly of Livingston, is, of course, did the experiment work?

The simple answer to that question is a resounding 'yes'. Even the most cynical of commentators would accept that the Livingston project 'worked'. Look around the town today. There's the huge retail centre that attracts visitors from all over the country. There are several sprawling industrial estates, there are sports, leisure and entertainment facilities. There are schools, a hospital, libraries, social-care facilities and places of worship. But above all, there are the people - Livingston's people. Whether first, second, third generation, newcomer, currently residing in or long since moved on, Livingston was made by its people. Not by the government, not by politicians, not by LDC, but by ITS PEOPLE.

Government and LDC and individual politicians between them devised and birthed the town, built its first houses and helped the town to take its first steps, but their only real lasting legacies are, for the most part, bricks and mortar, and roads. Without its people, Livingston would be nothing, and nowadays, Livingston IS its people.

The 'great experiment' worked, but that's not to say that everything happened just as was originally envisaged – far from it. In fact, in many ways, Livingston grew into the town it is today *in spite* of the government and LDC, rather than because of them. That in itself is in no way a slight on any politician or on LDC. Building a new-town and nursing it through its infancy had never really been attempted before the post WW2 era. LDC, the government and politicians were, in a sense, groping blindly, playing things by ear, so to speak. There was no real precedent in history to compare the project with, other than similar fledgling new-towns, and there was certainly no 'How to build and develop a completely new town with a largely immigrant population in five easy steps' handbook available to anyone. LDC were undoubtedly pioneers.

One myth about Livingston has endured since its inception, a myth that has been repeated so many times that people think of it as fact. That myth is that the town's population was, and is, mostly 'Glasgow Overspill'. That simply isn't the case. Yes, the town was built in part to provide housing for 'overspill' from cities like Glasgow, but LDC reports over the years, and census figures, tell the true story. Most people who moved to Livingston came from other areas of Lothian, that is, Edinburgh, Midlothian, East Lothian and the rest of West Lothian outwith Livingston's boundary. Inward migration from Glasgow rarely rose above 30% of the overall figure. Most Livingstonians came from Lothian itself, which isn't surprising, as many people from West Lothian's other towns, who would have lived in older mining houses, jumped at the chance of moving to a brand new house in the ever growing new-town on their doorstep- though in the very early days, many people from the outlying towns were apprehensive about the concrete colossus which was being constructed on their doorstep.

Livingston was by no means the first 'New Town' in the UK, nor was it the last. Wales has Cymbran and the aptly, but rather unimaginatively named, Newtown. England has Milton Keynes, Hastings, Northampton, Telford, Warrington and Peterborough. Scotland, in addition to Livingston, has Glenrothes, Irvine, East Kilbride and Cumbernauld. Another designated New-Town, Stonehouse, was never built. All of these towns, wherever they were in the UK, were built around much smaller existing clusters of settlements. Other settlements in the New-Town mould have been created since the 70's in England, but have been devised and designed completely differently from the towns that I just mentioned – in a sense, they are 'even- newer towns' and 'eco-towns'.

One political body, or group, who were responsible for almost killing Livingston, and who time and time again held back its development, were the Tories under Margaret Thatcher. No government has ever had such a negative effect on the town. The cuts after the Tory victory in 1979 effectively ended up holding back Livingston's social and economic development for ten, possibly even fifteen years. Livingston's two main founding aims on its inception were:

1.   To provide housing, particularly for 'overspill' population from Scotland's cities.

2.   To provide its people, and the locale, with new, <u>sustainable</u> jobs.

Aim one has been more or less accomplished. That is undeniable. Aim two never has been. A <u>sustainable</u> alternative to the area's old main industry, mining, has never been found, and for jobs, by and large, the town has relied on foreign owned companies setting up in the town for short to mid-term periods - though there have of course been a number of exceptions who have stayed and flourished- and more recently, on public-sector employment and on retail. For much of Livingston's lifespan, the percentage of foreign-owned companies occupying the town's industrial estates was as high as 89%. Some on

3

'the right' would argue that any jobs are good jobs, but as many people in Livingston will tell you, such a view is scant consolation to any worker who has been made redundant after five years with a foreign owned company in the town, when it decides to up-sticks and move to a different country because it's getting a better deal on corporation tax there, thus in many cases leaving the axed employees with skills only relevant to that departing company. The foreign factories have provided work for much of the town since its inception, but they should only ever have been a temporary solution to employment problems, they should never have become the vital umbilical cord upon which most people in the town relied to make a living. And this was mostly down to Thatcher's Tories.

I'm amazed that this hasn't been commented on in any of the previous books about the town. Livingston for many years was a great political irony. It had a hard-working, highly intelligent, much-respected MP in the form of Labour's Robin Cook, a man who worked tirelessly for the town, particularly where jobs were concerned, and the town itself had a workforce crying out for jobs, yet on so many occasions there was nothing Robin Cook could do when companies moved or closed on a whim, as his own party was in opposition while The Tories, far-off in London, wielded the axe over Scotland's economy and jobs with callous impunity because of the majority they had at Westminster all throughout the 80's and much of the 90's.

I won't over-politicise too much, but it should never be forgotten that the eighteen years of Tory rule from 1979 to 1997 saw their own heartland of south-east England boom, while Scotland, and Livingston, were practically left to rot. Whatever your viewpoint, you'd have to be wearing blue-tinted spectacles to think otherwise. The Conservative Party and Margaret Thatcher did Livingston and its people no favours, in fact, at one point, they wanted to do-away with Livingston altogether. Only intervention from some leading Scottish Tories and widespread outrage among other parties stopped Michael Heseltine, now a Tory Lord, from doing away with LDC and thus curtailing the town's further development – there was no sentimentality in this Tory U-Turn, retaining New Town status meant that Livingston would continue to receive vast amounts of infrastructure funding from the EEC/EU, which it would have lost without that New Town status, thus forcing central government to foot the bill for future development instead , and it's unlikely that they would have been so generous as the EEC/EU were. I make no apologies for highlighting the Tories' negative effect on the town – I grew up in the town and saw it with my own eyes and I'm sure most readers would agree, judging by how Livingston votes in elections– the town's voters are overwhelmingly of the Centre-Left.

The rate at which, in 1978, Livingston was predicted to create jobs, ended up falling well below 50 % of its target for most of the Tory years after they won in 1979. Thousands remained on the dole in 'Livi,' who would otherwise have been working. It took the town until the late 90's to really start to flourish again. But that's enough of politics for now.

Sport has been a big part of Livingston's story. Until the government and council in the last twenty years started fencing-off or selling off playing fields to build houses, Livingston had an abundance of places to play sport – particularly football. In addition to school playing fields, the town was blessed with many suitable green areas where football could be played, and most districts of the town also had some sort of all-weather kick-pitch. The trend of losing places to play football is a national one, not exclusive to Livingston, but it is worthwhile noting the decline in numbers of children playing football, and the failure of Scotland's Football Team to qualify for major tournaments since 1998, as both are undoubtedly linked. For many years, Livingston only had a junior side, Livingston United, but that all changed in the mid 1990's when struggling Meadowbank Thistle were re-franchised and moved to Livingston. They swiftly rose through the leagues, steadily rather than meteorically, and played their first match in Scotland's SPL in 2001 – a mere six years after they were 'reborn' as Livingston in what was then Division Three. To an outsider, having a professional team in the growing town might have seemed like a great idea, especially as they had an impressive new stadium at Almondvale. There was of course, one problem though. The vast majority of Livingstonians who followed football already supported Rangers, Celtic, Hibs, Hearts or some other established club. The old adage that says 'never trust someone who changes their football team' is perhaps a bit harsh in the Livingston context, but the truth is that the club suffered from a lack of support from fairly early on, once the curiosity of 'lapsed' Rangers and Celtic fans faded away, particularly as Livingston's rise coincided with Celtic's resurgence, meaning that many old-firm fans preferred to return to following the tried and tested 'two horse race'. No Livingstonian can be criticised for not flocking to the colours of the new club, football doesn't work like that. Though many football fans aim scorn at people who don't support their local team, in the case of Livingston, and that of other clubs who have relocated and refranchised to new-towns up and down the country, this scorn is virtually non-existent. Most of us already had a team when Livingston FC arrived on the scene.

Livingston FC did still enjoy some great initial successes, finishing third in the SPL in their first top-flight season and qualifying for the UEFA Cup, where they performed valiantly. Their greatest moment came in March 2004 at Hampden when, under the experienced Davie Hay, they beat Hibs 2-0 to win the Scottish League Cup. Since then, the club has been relegated, went bust and had to scale down drastically to survive, but there are green shoots of recovery at the club. What it achieved between 1995 and 2004 was simply incredible, given its humble beginnings.

The real life and soul of football in Livingston was, and probably always will be, its amateur, youth and children's teams. Murieston United in particular are a great example of a 'grass roots' success story.

Football isn't the only sport that has been part of Livingston New Town's story. Livingston has, or has had, swimming teams like the Dedridge Dolphins, a cricket club, a successful athletics club, a rugby club and even an American-Football Team and an Ice-Hockey team, as well as fairly successful archery and hockey clubs. There is also a multitude of bowling teams in the town. There was even a professional basketball team called MIM Livingston for a brief time.

The unsung heroes of sport in Livingston are the men and women who ran these clubs and teams, either as volunteers or as council or LDC employees. Their contribution to the town, and to its youth in particular, has been invaluable.

Livingston hasn't produced many big celebrities as such, but that's not to say that there haven't been any famous or notable people from the town. Most have been football players, which says a lot about what has already been discussed in this chapter. There has been Paul Dickov, who played at the highest level in England, and for Scotland, Gary Wales, best known for his spell at Hearts, Mark Burchill, formerly of Celtic and now assistant manager at Livingston, Scott Arfield, formerly a Falkirk player and Danny Wilson, who once played for Rangers. Going further back in time there were also Jimmy Scoular, who played at a high-level in England, and Tommy Walker, formerly of Hearts and Chelsea, both of whom came from the area.

James Mackenzie, the actor best known for presenting the kids TV show 'Raven', has a Livingston connection. Livingston and the surrounding area have produced several musical celebrities, the glaringly obvious example being Susan Boyle, the singer from nearby Blackburn who needs no introduction. There was also the highly talented singer and actress Kerry McGregor from Pumpherston and there was Cicero, the talented techno-popster who shot to fame in 1992. There have also been one or two musicians and performers from Scotland's rave-scene who lived in or near the town, who, like all of the town's other 'celebrities', played their part in giving Livingston a unique cultural identity.

Rave was big in Livingston. Between The Forum, The Bunker and nearby Ingliston, for a time in the 1990's there was practically an event of some sort every other week, and if there wasn't one nearby, there was always one somewhere else in Scotland. The rave scene is seen by some, mostly people who never went near one, as having been bad for Livingston and indeed for Scotland, primarily because of hysterical newspaper articles at the time, and the association with drugs and noise. I offer a different viewpoint that I'm sure most Livingstonians of a certain age would concur with. Rave brought Livingston's youth together. It gave them songs and a mini-sub-culture of their own, which was totally divorced from that of their parents and thus gave them their own identity. Rave also had an unexpected, positive social effect on the town and surrounding area. Of course, not everyone in Livingston was into rave music, and rave brought with it drugs and criminality, and some sad, untimely deaths, but the drugs, criminality and small number of tragic deaths, though regrettable, could just as easily have occurred without the rave scene. People will always want to get off their faces as long as there is boredom or misery in society.

Until the early 90's, it is widely accepted that Livingston, though a de-facto single town, was actually a collection of smaller new-villages, connected by underpasses and foot-bridges. No more so is this symbolised than by the intermittent 'gang warfare' that existed between the town's districts. Deans fought Knightsridge. Knightsridge fought Ladywell. Ladywell fought Craigshill. Craigshill, surrounded as it was, fought Howden, Ladywell, East/Mid Calder and Pumpherston. At times, Livingston's districts 'teamed up' to fight youths from Bathgate and other places. In most cases, this 'warfare' within Livingston consisted of large gangs of youths, males and females usually of all ages from about twelve to eighteen, who would gather on 'their' district's side of the underpass or footbridge and chase and goad their counterparts on the 'other side' of an evening. Though there were some serious assaults, fights and even attempted murders over the many years that this went on for, for the most part, chasing each other back and forth was about as much as most of the youths did. This kind of behaviour often drew police attention, and re-affirmed many young Livingstonians' sense of dentity – you were from Craigshill/Ladywell/ Howden/Knightsridge first, Livingston second. Sometimes the crowds of youths glaring at each other over the foot-bridges and underpasses would number in the hundreds. This can be explained by two simple facts – there was a larger than normal population of youth in the town compared to the national average, and for a long time, especially in the Tory years, youths and older kids had nothing to do at night.

Three things stopped, or at least, drastically scaled down this type of thing in the 1990's. Rave played a big part, especially with the slightly older youths, as they started to meet, have fun with, and even go out with, boys and girls from other districts that they had met and got to know at raves. Secondly, the closure of Craigshill High School, which effectively threw most of the youths from four of the competing areas into one-school, and thus within only a year or two, most of the kids had realised that they weren't different to each other, drastically reducing this 'gang warfare' further. Thirdly, and perhaps more obviously, as youths in Livingston left school and began to work beside, study beside and drink with people from other areas of the town, the hostility that some felt towards other districts largely faded, and became absurd to most. That's not to say that 'that type of thing' vanished from Livingston completely, but it has never re-occurred on anything like the same scale since the 80's and 90's, and such incidents have become isolated. It is also worth noting that this type of 'gang warfare' happens between youths all over the world, the youths weren't doing anything that their peers across the globe didn't also do.

The same can be said of drugs and vandalism. Though they have been the scourge of Livingston at times, they are the scourge of any county, town, city or village, and these problems are human problems, not Livingston problems.

Scotland's sectarianism issues inevitably followed people into Livingston, but have never really been a big problem in the town, at least, not on the scale that they have been elsewhere in Scotland. There have been plenty of orange walks and Irish nights in the town, but they've caused no more trouble than local pubs or clubs have on a regular basis at chucking-out time. Despite large numbers of Livingstonians supporting Rangers or Celtic, for the most part, people live and work beside each other irrespective of faith or politics. Livingston, by and large, in time has rejected sectarianism, and that is something that both the town and its people can be proud of. We are all Livingstonians, be we blue, green, red, orange, white or black.

Livingston certainly hasn't wanted for culture and entertainment over the years. Groups like West Lothian Youth Theatre, now called 'Firefly', offered fantastic opportunities for some of the town's creative youth, and produced some great stage shows. Groups like The Livingston Players have offered opportunities for adults to participate in drama and productions too. There have also been brass-bands, skateboard clubs, moped clubs, fishing clubs, army and air cadets, majorettes troupes, orange bands, pipe bands, a few minor rock-bands who were only famous in the locale, and a multitude of pubs to go to as well.

The biggest difference between old Livingston and Livingston today is, of course, the fact that it now has something resembling a proper town centre. In bygone days, though there were one or two pubs at The Centre, it generally wasn't the place to be at weekends or in the evenings. Now there are a Boulevard, a cinema, pubs and restaurants there, meaning that The Centre really IS a proper town-centre now. It's sad that this was one of the last pieces of the Livingston puzzle to fall into place, but at least it is there now- better late than never. Most of Britain's other new-towns had the same problem for years too.

Livingston is now a 'real' town, rather than the aggregate of communities that it once was, and this has been accomplished by Livingston's people, with a little help from Mr. Brick and Mr. Mortar of course. Towns, like nations and indeed individuals, are, to a certain degree, responsible for their own transgression. Be proud. YOU made Livingston what it is today. YOU played your part, and it's YOU and YOUR children who will make its future and share some of the responsibility, and the credit, for its future success.

Livingston has had its tragedies and its miracles, its openings and closures, its jobs boosts and lay-offs, its battles and reconciliations, its constructions and demolitions, its share of boom and bust, its assaults, crimes, accidents and vandalisms, its good people and its not so good people, hard-working politicians who worked tirelessly for the town and greedy self-serving charlatans who were only in politics to line their pockets. There has been sadness, joy, life and death, love, hate and laughter. There have been events to bring a tear to the eye, some that would bring sorrow to the heart, some that would have the average Livingstonian scratching his or her head in confusion, and some that would have those same Livingstonians wetting themselves with laughter. As in every other town, something different occurs every day, affecting someone, or something. Here, on a day by day basis, is a written kaleidoscope of some of the sad, weird and wonderful things that have happened in Livingston over the years, 'On This Day'...

JANUARY

Monday 1st January 1996.
Five people from West Lothian and Livingston were honoured in the Queen's new-year list. Golfer Bernard Gallacher, originally from Bathgate, was awarded an OBE. LDC's own Jim Pollok was given a CBE for his services to industry. Alison Davies, Scotland's representative for Save The Children, was given an OBE in recognition of over thirteen years of sterling work for that charity and others, while Charge-Nurse Flora Brodie, known locally as 'Sister Flo', was honoured with an MBE for twenty-seven years of service at Bangour and St John's Hospitals. The final award went to Bathgate-born John Og, who was given The Queen's Police Medal. He is best remembered for thwarting an attempted arms smuggling operation by UVF fanatics in Falkirk the previous year.

Wednesday 2nd January 1985.
Livingston's Rate-payers' new Rates came into effect, with a staggering rise of 20%, that it was feared would push many into poverty. The increase had been due to take effect the previous April but had been delayed by West Lothian Council for as long as possible, given the economic climate at the time. Rate-payers were urged to write letters of complaint to The Secretary of State for Scotland. Rates were later abolished and replaced by the 'Community Charge' or 'Poll Tax', and Scotland was used as a Guinea-Pig for the new unfair tax before it was rolled out across Britain.

Friday 3rd January 1992.
The Archbishop of Edinburgh, Keith O'Brien, now Cardinal O'Brien and former head of the Catholic Church in Scotland , made a public statement slamming planned school closures in West Lothian as 'deplorable', particularly the 'wholly arbitrary decision' to close St Kenneth's RC in Knightsridge, which he described as a

11

viable school. He also vowed to have a 'showdown' with Scottish Secretary Ian Lang, who was the man widely accepted to have been behind all of West Lothian's school closures at that time.

Wednesday 3rd January 1996.

Livingston Police launched 'Operation Trawl', a campaign designed to clamp down on drunk-driving and un-roadworthy vehicles. The massive operation eventually saw some 8000 cars pulled over and checked, only six of whose drivers were found to be under the influence of alcohol – better figures than almost anywhere else in the UK. Police seized a number of 'un-roadworthy' vehicles, but later said that their efforts had been hampered by snow and bad weather, which would have kept many 'dodgy' cars off the road, and thus unable to be checked. All in all, the operation was, statistically, a great success.

Saturday 4th January 1992.

Detectives were investigating the remains of a woman, found that morning in the grounds of the old Bangour Hospital. A walker, who was collecting logs in the grounds, alerted the police after seeing a human skull sticking out of the ground. Police were as yet unsure of the cause of death, as it was clear even from early examinations that the woman, aged between 35 and 45, had laid there for about five years. Police refused to rule out murder, as the only clothing found near the gruesome discovery had been a few items of women's underwear.

Friday 5th January 1996.

A thirty-seven year-old Bingo-caller from the town appeared on Channel 4's quiz show 'Backdate', which was hosted by Valerie Singleton. The Bingo-Caller, Murray Spiers, was a member of MENSA and was expected to do well in the contest, having easily qualified for the show after an audition in Edinburgh.

Sunday 6th January 1985.

Scottish Residential unveiled a new development of private-housing for sale at Mid Calder called 'The Paddock'. Standard features on all housing included garage, central heating, wall tiling in the bathroom, a free doorbell, a bare but seeded front lawn, stained wood windows, solid timber front doors and coloured bathroom suites.

The different houses available in the development were priced as follows:

One- bedroom house - £20,900
Two-bedroom bungalow - £32,750
Two-bedroom villa – £35,950
Three-bedroom villa - £45,750
Four-bedroom detached cottage - £52,950

Thursday 7th January 2010.

The 'Courier reported that Livingston Designer Outlet was closed temporarily, citing health and safety concerns related to the snowy conditions. Shoppers had contacted the 'Courier to inform them that stores at the outlet had been very cold and that buckets had been put out to catch water leaking from pipes. In some cases, shop staff were wearing gloves while working indoors, before the centre finally gave in and closed. It was not known when it would re-open. This happened amid the second 'big freeze' in as many years. Livingston has always suffered badly due to heavy snow, as its housing and industrial estates are more widely-scattered than they are in Scotland's cities, meaning there is less of a concentration of heat from buildings, thus the snow is more likely to lie.

Thursday 8th January 1987.

Uniroyal at nearby Newbridge opened its new £10m extension to its tyre-making plant. Two Livingston men, who had been long-term unemployed before being given jobs at the plant, were given the honour of opening the extension. In the previous six-years, the workforce at the plant had increased by 23%. The plant later became Continental Tyres and was, thanks to its unions, one of the best-paying places to work in the locale if you were a semi-skilled or unskilled worker. It closed in late 1999, production moving to Eastern Europe as the firm looked to save money.

Tuesday 8ᵗʰ January 1991.

A lorry crashed into the heavy school gates at Mid Calder Primary School, damaging them severely and forcing council staff to move one of the 280lb gates out of the way, propping it against a barrier near the school's entrance. Bungling council staff then forgot all about the gate, and a few days later it almost decapitated a teacher when it fell after snagging on her bag. Still, the gate was not fixed or moved, and two months later, the gate caught in a ten year-old girl's swimming bag, falling onto her head. The little girl received a nasty head wound and was said by medics to be 'lucky to be alive'. Later, an outraged Sheriff at Linlithgow blasted the council, saying 'there were no excuses where the safety of children is concerned', as he imposed a fine of £1000 on the council for the incidents.

Tuesday 9ᵗʰ January 2007.

A Royal Marine from Livingston, serving in Afghanistan, had his life saved by a new military vehicle which shrugs off direct hits by explosives. The 12.5 ton Viking BVS10 armoured vehicle, which was on its first operational tour, could roar up a 45-degree incline with ease, be parachuted ready-to-use into war zones and could even manoeuver in water. The twenty-four year-old soldier said 'We were under-fire when enemy mortars landed just two metres away from my Viking and there wasn't even a scratch on her. Small arms fire rounds just bounced off her like stone chippings.' A British forces hardware expert later said 'considerably more' troops would have died in the attack, if it had not been for the new vehicles, which cost £1m each.

Friday 10ᵗʰ January 1975.

Livingston's six-a-side football league unveiled its new honorary president, Linlithgow-born former Hearts and Scotland star Donald Ford. He instantly appealed for more committee members, as at the time there were only eight of them, while the league itself had just under 800 participants.

Tuesday 11th January 2011.
Police appealed for witnesses and information after two local businesses under common ownership were the subject of suspicious fire-attacks in the early hours of the morning. No-one was injured in the blazes, but both Grand Central in Carmondean and Howden Chippy were severely damaged. Police were sure that the two incidents were linked.

Tuesday 12th January 1988.
An Ambulance Driver from Howden , who had just ran the Falkirk half-marathon, announced that he had raised enough sponsorship money to equip all of West Lothian's ambulances with vital mobile diagnostic equipment. The man, George Miller, who was the training instructor at the local ambulance station, said that he had been 'bitten by the running bug' and that his next target was to raise £4000 to buy a vital defibrillator for the station, this time at the Dundee and Ayr half-marathons. His initial target when he first began fundraising had been a mere £200. At the time, the Livingston ambulance station responded to over 500 calls a month, and the equipment bought using the money George raised saved many lives in Livingston. Livingston had eight ambulances at the time, seven on constant standby, with one in reserve. West Lothian had fourteen in total

Wednesday 13th January 1988.
Livingston MP Robin Cook described as 'bizarre' the situation regarding the future of Livingston's giant Gateway Store, whose owners, The Dee Corporation, were at the time subject to a takeover bid from a 'confectionary company'. Mr. Cook offered The Dee Corporation 'every political assistance' on the condition that they relinquished their lease on the Fine Fare unit, which was lying empty and useless. On the same day, the MP also had a meeting with the Centre's management, to discuss the problem of children and youths fighting over trolleys in the multi-storey and underground car-parks, and to have a meeting regarding a possible new occupant for the Fine Fare unit, which many believed was being deliberately left empty by Gateway's owners in a bid to keep competitors out. At the same

meeting, it emerged that Tesco or ASDA were the front-runners to take over Livingston's Gateway, in the event of the aforementioned takeover going ahead.

Sunday 14th January 1968.

Livingston suffered one of the worst storms ever recorded in the town, which actually lasted until well into the next day. On the Monday morning, residents woke to find the streets littered with debris, and several houses, mostly in Craigshill, actually had their roofs blown off by the fierce gales. Immediate steps were taken by LDC to repair and clean up the damage.

Wednesday 14th January 1987.

Twenty jobs were axed at Cameron Iron Works, in addition to the 114 jobs that had already been lost at the plant the previous October. The job losses were blamed on the global oil-slump. These lay-offs took the workforce there down to 730. At its peak, the plant had employed over 1200 people.

Tuesday 15th January 1985.

The Public Roads Safety Department in Livingston announced in its annual report that twenty-two people had been killed on the district's roads in the previous year. The worst place for road-accidents in the last year had been Livingston, with 380 accidents, while Bathgate was close behind with 336. Bridgend was declared the safest, where there had only been four accidents. Two-wheeled road users had faired particularly badly – with eight motorcyclists and three pedal-cyclists being killed, in addition to a further 141 motor and pedal bike users being injured. Livingston police said that in truth, in most cases, there was no such thing as an accident, as someone was almost always to blame for a crash, either through bad judgment and/or carelessness.

Thursday 16th January 1975.

LDC announced the commencement of work on a new training facility in the town, concerned with the drilling for and production of oil, amid the North-Sea oil-boom. Located in Deans Industrial Estate, plans were already in motion for a full-sized 'Rig' platform to be brought to the site from England, to make training as realistic as possible. It was to open that summer and was initially run by the Petroleum Industry Training Board. The project was around 75% funded by public money, by deed of a series of grants and loans from The Manpower Services Commission.

Tuesday 17th January 2012.

A Livingston shop-keeper was ambushed by a masked robber wielding an eight-inch meat cleaver, after a fake call in the middle of the night to tell him his burglar alarm was going off. As the shop-keeper arrived at the Ladywell Foodstore in Thymebank and opened up, the robber pounced and demanded 'cash and fags immediately'. He escaped with more than £5000 and around 8000 cigarettes after smashing open a cabinet and safe. The shop-keeper, though clearly shaken, was not injured in the robbery, and police appealed for information.

Wednesday 18th January 1978.

A cartoon character named 'Mr. Sporty' was officially adopted by Livingston and District Sports Council as their mascot. Mr. Sporty looked like a cross between Willy Wonka and one of the 'Mr. Men' from children's' books. He was created to help promote the idea of sport for all the family in the town, and the decision to adopt him was unanimous both among local community groups and the LDC.

Sunday 18th January 2009.

A charity dinner at the Raj Poot Restaurant in Pumpherston, intended to raise funds to send humanitarian aid to the beleaguered people of Gaza and attended by Livingston's MP and its MSP, found itself targeted by a mob of moronic protestors carrying Union Jacks and Israel flags, chanting 'Terrorists go home', 'Fuck the Pope' and 'No Surrender' at guests as they arrived for the dinner, which raised £30,000 for the worthwhile humanitarian cause. MSP Angela Constance was particularly disgusted by the actions of the thugs, as there were around thirty children present at the dinner. MP Jim Devine received nuisance phone calls from some of the bigots involved in the protest in the run up to the event, and described them as 'bully boys'. Quick witted police, forewarned of the 'protest', made no arrests and kept the angry mob on the other side of the road from the restaurant.

Thursday 19th January 1978.
A man from Craigshill appeared at West Lothian District Court, charged with 'creating a public nuisance' by urinating in the street. As the accused already had a previous conviction for the same offence, he was fined £2, and given fourteen days in which to pay said fine.

Wednesday 20th January 1988.
The announcement was made that there were now no rats in the former Fine-Fare Superstore's empty building. A local councilor had contacted environmental health officials following several rodent sightings at the building. However, environmental health officers on this day said that the rats were gone. The rats had been living in Fine Fare's cardboard compactor, which had not been emptied when the store was hastily closed.

Monday 21st January 1985.
Woolco in The Centre began its much advertised bicycle sale, with the following offers:
Compact GL Unisex three-speed folding cycle - £49.95 – reduced from £79.95
Blazer GT BMX with 20" black wheels and red pads - £64.95 – reduced from 89.95
Hustler BMX with 16" wheels and yellow pads   £49.95 – reduced from £69.95.
Further £10 reductions were also available on Racers, BMXs, Unisex bikes and children's bikes.

Friday 21st January 2011.
The Tower in Craigshill played host to a concert by world-famous Celtic band, Charlie and the Bhoys, after the band's Celtic supporters' function, originally planned for a venue in Bathgate, had

to be moved at the last minute after threats from bigots and complaints from locals. The Tower gig went ahead without any hitches or disruption, and a great night was had by all.

Thursday 22nd January 1987.

Described as a 'National Scandal' by MP Robin Cook, crisp manufacturer Golden Wonder announced that they were closing their plant at Broxburn, with the eventual loss of 341 jobs. Robin Cook said that he was 'disgusted' by the behaviour of the company, whom he accused of asset-stripping. The plant had recently received around £750,000 in public money, part of which had been used to buy updated machinery, which Golden Wonder later moved to its production facility south of the border.

Friday 23rd January 1998.

A ghost tour in the Royal Mile area of Edinburgh was confronted by an angry Livingston couple whose baby they had wakened, Edinburgh Sheriff Court heard. The baby's father appeared on the scene brandishing a meat cleaver. His partner had already been fined £80 for the incident, but the man, from Deans, had been on bail at the time and was thus given a three-month jail term for breach of the peace. Some people on the 'ghost tour' reportedly thought that the Livingston couple were part of the tour.

Tuesday 24th January 1978.

A woman from Craigshill became Lothian's first ever female school janitor. She took up the role at Craigshill High School, where she had previously been employed as a cleaner. Her 'boss', the school's head-janitor, later commented that she had taken well to her new role and was now an invaluable member of the team.

Wednesday 25th January 1980.

Livingston Police issued a stern public warning, chiefly aimed at people who lived in what was then the Murieston area, but also generally meant for the ears of everyone in the town. The warning concerned supermarket shopping-trolleys being dumped all over the town, which police said was dangerous and wasteful of their time.

Concerned citizens had reported seeing gangs of youths jubilantly hurling the trolleys into the River Almond, and cheering enthusiastically as they hit the water. Some trolleys were found miles away from the centre, near the sewage works beside what is now Almondell Country Park, which would suggest that kids were going to Herculean lengths to leave the trolleys in the most ridiculous of places.

Sunday 25th January 1985.

Livingston scored a triple-success, with individual entrants from the town claiming 1st, 2nd and 3rd places in a national championship. The event they triumphed at was the World Haggis Eating Championships, held in Corby, Northamptonshire. The champion, Peter McPhee, received £100 in cash and a gallon of whisky, which he said would be raffled for charity, then announced that his next challenge would be trying to break the world record for eating raw eggs, at an event to be held soon in Craigshill Social Club.

Sunday 26th January 1992.

Animal welfare officers in Livingston were sickened by a discovery in a park in the town. An Old English sheepdog was found tied to a tree and apparently left to die in its own filth in Craigshill's Almond Park. In its emaciated and depressed state, the poor animal had been reduced to eating bones, plastic and rubbish to keep itself alive. The SSPCA referred to the incident as 'the worst case of animal cruelty that they had ever seen', but were hopeful that the dog could be saved. They appealed for anyone who had information about the dog's owner to contact them.

Wednesday 27th January 1988.

At around 6pm, a Vauxhall car was travelling along Houston Road when a three-foot stake was dropped onto it by vandals from the Ladywell-Knightsridge footbridge. The roof of the car was seriously damaged and the windscreen was completely smashed, but miraculously, the car's three occupants, though badly shaken, were not seriously injured. The Police caught the boy who actually threw the stake, and a report was submitted about him to The Children's' Panel.

Thursday 28th January 1823.

Reverend Robertson at Livingston Kirk sent a letter to Lord Hopetoun, expressing his concern that the cemetery that he was responsible for may be targeted by body-snatchers, as part of the lucrative but illegal trade in human cadavers for experimental science. Robertson even requested permission to employ an armed guard at the graveyard, a practice common in Edinburgh's cemeteries at the time.

Tuesday 29th January 2002.

Livingston received a major jobs boost as HMRC announced plans to open a new office and call centre in the town, at Silverburn House. Initially some 360 employees would soon move into the 30,000 square- foot office at Almondvale Business Park, which had been given a twenty-one year lease. It was a positive development, in the wake of a recent spate of factory closures in and around the town.

Tuesday 30th January 1978.

The huge, iconic concrete cow that sat outside The Lanthorn was temporarily removed back to Bloom Farm to have its broken ears and tail repaired, having been vandalised. The artist who created the cow expected the repairs to take around one week to complete. Concrete Sheep were installed as a temporary replacement, and they themselves have become as iconic to the people of Livingston as The Centre itself.

Monday 31st January 2011.

A Livingston motorist was jailed after he was caught driving while disqualified for the 18th time. On seventeen of those occasions, he had also been driving with no insurance. The Sheriff at Livingston Court jailed the twenty-six year-old man for ten months and banned him from driving for ten years.

FEBRUARY

Wednesday 1st February 2012.
A local fifty-one year-old man who inherited a revolver as a family memento was spared the minimum five-year jail sentence for illegally possessing a gun. He was a schoolboy when he was given the Belgian weapon, which had belonged to his grandfather who served with distinction during the First World War. Police had found the old revolver while at the man's house investigating another matter. Due to the exceptional circumstances, he was ordered to carry out 150 hours of unpaid community work.

Thursday 2nd February 1978.
Vandals broke into Almondbank Primary School in Craigshill, after smashing a window on the school's west side. Almost all of the school's classroom doors and locked cupboards were forced open, and a small sum of money was also stolen from the school. As a result of this, Lothian's Director of Education announced that all schools in the area would be tightening up on security, though he confessed that this itself could be problematic as no-one could predict which school would be the next target. No-one was ever caught for this particular break-in.

Tuesday 3rd February 2004.
A pitiful crowd of just 6601 at neutral Easter Road saw Livingston narrowly edge out Dundee 1-0 in the League Cup Semi-Final, thanks to a late penalty from Derek Lilley. The Lions would face either Rangers or Hibernian in the final.

Saturday 4th February 1996.
Livingston was said to be 'flooded with counterfeit money' as police appealed on the radio for the public to be extra vigilant. The notes were mostly Bank of England £20 notes of 'fairly poor quality', and the public were reminded that to pass-on or attempt to pass-on such notes was a criminal offence, even if they themselves

were unaware that the money was counterfeit. Shopkeepers were advised to use detector-pens and to look out for the watermark in the forged notes. In the end, some fifteen arrests were made in connection with this episode.

Tuesday 5th February 2002.

A former SNP parliamentary candidate, who taught Modern Studies at Inveralmond High School, was sacked by the school after becoming the centre of a sexual-misconduct case regarding Inveralmond students. The education board dismissed the more serious charges against him, but sacked him for failing to keep a professional distance from his students. He had been suspended from the school on full pay since 1999. Police had earlier dropped criminal charges against the teacher, who had also been the subject of a similar complaint in 1998. The teacher consistently protested his innocence and blamed a conspiracy against him, caused by his threatening to speak out about supposed violent behaviour of students towards teachers at the badly failing school. As a result of the allegations, he had been assaulted twice and threatened twice by pupils, while his car had also been vandalised. He was never accused of actually having sex with students. Inveralmond Community High School had been dogged by reports of bullying, stories of drug dealing in the car park, assaults on teachers and widespread sexual misconduct. Persistent under-achievement in exams, and abysmal truancy figures, despite cash injections from the Scottish Executive, had also been highlighted.

Wednesday 6th February 2013.

The last staff left Halls in Broxburn as the plant finally closed forever. There had been a steady stream of pay-offs since the plant had announced its closure the previous October. Several attempts to save the eighty-year-old business had ended in failure, and in total, 1700 workers lost their jobs, in what was a tragic economic blow not just for Broxburn and Livingston, but for Scotland as a whole. The plant had been bought by a huge multi-national corporation a few years before, and this corporation, Vion, had closed the plant claiming that it was losing too much money. The actual brand name of Halls has since been bought by a smaller competitor, who managed to find jobs for around fifty of Halls' drivers- but the Broxburn site itself was not part of their plans. Not for the first time, Livingston and West Lothian's workers suffered as a result of a foreign owned company ceasing operations in the area with little or no notice.

Sunday 7th February 1988.
Youngsters from the Open Door homeless hostel in Craigshill wrote a letter to Richard Branson, the millionaire boss of 'Virgin', asking for funds to provide them with a mini-bus and recreational facilities for the project. The youngsters were hopeful that the tycoon would be sympathetic to their cause. An Open Door spokesman confirmed in an additional letter that they needed money to buy a variety of other things too, including a decent cooker and some furniture. He also commended the youngsters for their efforts. Sadly, no mini-bus was ever provided.

Wednesday 8th February 2006.
Livingston suffered their worst ever competitive defeat, going down 7-0 to Hibernian at Easter Road. The season would bring relegation, and a record of the worst final points total in the history of the SPL to date, though Gretna later managed to do even worse in season 07-08.

Sunday 9th February 1992.
Livingston's first and only male pop-star, Dave Cicero or just 'Cicero', peaked at number 19 in the UK charts with his electro-pop single 'Love is Everywhere'. He had also reached number eight in the Scottish Charts. The video for the single was mostly filmed under the dual-carriageway in Livingston ,with cameo appearances from Cicero's friends, many of whom were well-known lads from Craigshill. Livingston's first 'celebrity', he was snubbed by Top of the Pops, but performed his catchy track in front of millions of viewers on the Saturday TV show 'Motormouth'. He had been discovered a few years previously, after handing a demo-tape to The Pet Shop Boys at one of their gigs. They were so impressed that they

made him the first signing to their new record label 'Spaghetti Records', produced his first songs, and Neil Tennant even performed backing vocals on 'Love is Everywhere', which was actually Cicero's second single and was his only big hit. Cicero supported Take That on their 1992 UK tour.

Wednesday 9th February 2000.

Property consultants NAI Gooch Webster were involved in two large-scale industrial deals at Livingston which would bring hundreds of much-needed jobs to the town. In the first transaction, the 170,000 sq ft former Wincanton distribution depot at Houston Industrial Estate changed hands. The facility was acquired by M&S Toiletries, which took a 10-year lease on the premises at an initial rent of £525,000 per annum. M&S Toiletries would relocate from its dilapidated facility at Sighthill Industrial Estate on the west side of Edinburgh. That same day, in one of Scotland's biggest industrial deals for years, Halifax plc paid £4m for the former Unisys facility, a 200,000 sq ft unit at Baird Road in Kirkton Campus. Some 50% of the building was at the time leased by Jabil Circuit. Halifax upgraded the remaining space for use as a back-up to its recently announced banking centre in Edinburgh.

Sunday 10th February 1991.

After spending the weekend with her beloved sister Sharon in Livingston, 15-year-old Vicky Hamilton went missing. She was last seen waiting for a bus in nearby Bathgate.

Saturday 11th February 1978.

Livingston got its first indoor skateboard rink, opened by the town's only skateboard club, The Skate Cats. Located in an outbuilding of Craigsfarm, it was initially proposed that the rink would only be open at weekends, to capitalise on the sport's growing popularity. Its ramp was constructed by Newhailes Plastics of Edinburgh. The building itself would later become The Playshed, and then the home of West Lothian Youth Theatre. At the opening ceremony, an LDC official confirmed that talks were also in progress regarding a possible outdoor skateboard rink in the town, and that full details would be available soon.

Friday 12th February 1988.
Scotland's first epilepsy centre specifically for children was opened by Gordon Stark, a leading pediatrician from Bangour. The new centre, in Dedridge, was to provide information and advice for parents of children with epilepsy, and would initially be open for three days a week. Such was the demand for the new centre, that it received twelve applications to join and use it before it was even advertised.

Wednesday 13th February 1985.
LDC overwhelmingly rejected proposals from chemical and gas giant Union Carbide, who wanted to build a huge production facility in the town. A strong campaign by the people of Livingston helped make LDC's decision for them, though Union Carbide were allowed to operate a small retail-only unit in Houston Industrial Estate. The company would have brought hundreds of jobs to the town, but no-one wanted them in Livingston, as they had only a year previously killed 3000 people and injured some 400,000 more when their plant at Bhopal in India had exploded and then suffered a major toxic gas-leak.

Friday 14th February 1992.
Cinema goers in Livingston looking for a romantic Valentine's Day movie at Livingston's two-screen cinema were to be sorely disappointed by what was showing. Screen One was showing 'Bill and Ted's Bogus Journey' , while Screen Two was showing 'The Addams Family' – two films more suited to Halloween. Those movie-lovers who traveled to Bathgate cinema in search of something more romantic were also to be disappointed, as it was showing a Disney cartoon called 'The Rescuers Down Under'.

Wednesday 15th February 1978.
Livingston suffered its coldest day weather-wise since records began. The temperature recorded was just 18.2 degrees Centigrade.

Thursday 16th February 1978.

Pupils at Letham Primary School were said to be 'in tears' as they stood in the playground in the freezing cold, after an odd decision by the school's Headmaster to have them wait outside because the school's heating was broken. Furious parents later arranged a meeting to discuss the incident, and a complaint was made to the local education authority.

Friday 17th February 1979.

The town of Livingston made its first appearance on national TV since a broadcast from Riverside Primary some years before. The Trim Course beside the Almond was featured on the BBC's 'Spectrum' show, with every 'obstacle' on the now largely redundant training course being shown, and their designs analysed.

Thursday 18th February 1988.

At a meeting of LDC's main board, there was widespread embarrassment as members considering an application to build a petrol-station at the Lizzie Bryce Roundabout realised that none of them had a clue who Lizzie Bryce actually was. Some thought she was a 12th century character, others that she had been a local witch in the 16th century. In truth she was just a local woman who kept animals, and she was born in 1776 and died in 1865. She lived in a house with her daughter near what is now the Mid Calder side of the Dedridge footbridge that crosses the dual-carriageway. No sign of her house remains today, but there are traces of her sheep-dip and her gamekeeper's house a few hundred yards from the modern footbridge. Despite naming a roundabout and a pub in Dedridge (now demolished) after her, none of the red-faced LDC officials knew who she was. She was not a witch.

Wednesday 19th February 1969.

A statement regarding the imminent opening of Livingston's first Catholic Church, St Andrews in Craigshill, was released by the Catholic Press Office. It explained that the new church's distinctive architecture was specifically designed to contrast nicely with existing buildings in Craigshill, and that the unique design of the church meant that no congregation member within would ever be more than forty-five feet from the altar. Still in use today, from the air, the structure looks like a fish, the early symbol of Christian unity in the days when Christians were persecuted by pagans, and this was also a very deliberate architectural choice.

Friday 20th February 1987.

Around 250 students at Craigshill High School had to be evacuated when the floor collapsed in the school's main-hall during a concert by Scots folk-legends The Battlefield Band. The cause of the collapse was said to be dry rot in the floor supports. Thankfully, no-one was injured. Not for the first or last time, the school's dilapidated state made the headlines.

Sunday 21st February 1971.

Knightsridge House, the two-storey stately home originally built for Alexander Gray of Heiff in 1851, was officially given category B listed-building status at a small ceremony, on what was by all accounts, a freezing day.

Friday 21st February 1992.

A Livingston company announced that they had invented a new 'green' gel for use with hospital ultrasound machines and in industry, which they hoped would greatly expand their international sales and bring dozens of jobs to the town. The company, Diagnostic Sonar Ltd, claimed that their new gel was a marked improvement on existing gels as not only did it allow for clearer scanning, it was also far less likely to cause skin irritation than its competitors' brands. Variants of this gel are still in use in hospitals today.

Friday 22nd February 1985.

Brown Asbestos was removed from Almondbank Primary School in Craigshill. It had been feared that the substance, discovered a fortnight earlier during renovation work, would seriously endanger the lives of the schoolchildren, as well as those who used the resource centre and library. Craigshill Community Council publicly declared that 'all children in Craigshill were now safe from Asbestos'.

Tuesday 23rd February 1988.
Craigsfarm's manager John Hoey proclaimed 'everything must go' as he opened the community centre's sale. At the time, the roofs were being removed from the farm buildings as part of ongoing renovations, and literally everything inside had to be disposed of. At the time, it was the biggest sale ever held at any community centre in Livingston. Beds went for only £10, three-piece sofas sold for £15 and there were numerous other bargains including 'pot luck' lucky bags containing household goods to be had.

Saturday 24th February 1978.
Livingston's 'Miracle' Priest, Father Byrne, died aged 59 at Edinburgh's St Raphael's Hospital. He was Livingston's first ever Catholic Priest. He had been ordained at St Patrick's in County Carlow, Ireland, in 1945. He was much liked and respected by most people of all faiths in Livingston and was said to have been a 'leading light in the diocese'.

Saturday 25th February 1978.
The Linlithgow and Stirlingshire Foxhound Association held a huge Fox-Hunt near Dedridge, with several poor defenceless Foxes being torn apart. This barbaric 'sport' was finally outlawed in 1997 by the new Labour Government, though the decision was just as much about politics as it was about animal welfare.

Friday 26th February 1982.
Workers and Shop Stewards from the Plessey Capacitor Factory at Bathgate were at Edinburgh High Court, where a decision made three weeks previously, ordering the mostly female workforce to end its occupation of the doomed facility, was reversed.

Tuesday 27th February 1973.
Livingston's first Roman Catholic Primary School was opened in the town, at St Andrews, Howden, with facilities to teach up to 500

pupils. Before it opened, RC pupils had been schooled at existing non-denominational school facilities in East Calder and Craigshill.

Tuesday 28th February 2006.

The generous staff and customers of Livingston's Vue Cinema, having raised £5000 for Guide Dogs for the Blind, presented a donation of a fully-trained guide-dog to the charity, after a small afternoon ceremony at the popular new cinema.

Thursday 29th February 1996.

Maintenance workers at Halls in Broxburn defiantly stated that their wage-dispute with the company would go on, as their industrial action entered its fourth week. The dispute had arisen because the factory's few-dozen maintenance workers had been given a 1.5% wage rise, while the factory's 1000 process operators had been given a 6% pay rise. After negotiation, Halls agreed to also give a 6% rise to the maintenance workers on the condition that they scrapped their tea breaks. At that point, the electricians and engineers left the talks, and the dispute rumbled on.

MARCH

Monday 1st March 1976.
LDC celebrated the letting of the town's 7000th house, to a young couple with children who had moved all the way from Cornwall.

Tuesday 2nd March 1992.
A treasurer of a football supporters club appeared in court accused of stealing over £1000 from Deans and District Rangers Supporters Club. The man, from Deans, admitted stealing the money between October and November the previous year. At the time of the court appearance he hadn't yet paid any of the stolen money back, so sentencing was deferred, though the Sheriff indicated that community service may be his next step.

Friday 3rd March 1989.
A social study's results were published, revealing that there were now 916 single-parent households in Livingston, 6.7% of households in the town, with 1636 children living with just one parent or guardian. It also revealed that in total, Livingston had 1.8 children per-household.

Friday 4th March 1988.
A Livingston family appeared in the papers, revealing that they had been left with soaking carpets for over six months, largely thanks to the installation of slanted roofs in Craigshill. The family had been given just one dust-sheet by the inept builders to cover their carpets, and were greatly concerned about damp, particularly as they had a little boy to look after. The family understandably said that they were considering legal action against the bungling council to recover damages caused by the leaking-water.

Tuesday 5th March 1996.
The West Lothian Awards, in conjunction with the 'Courier, were held at Howden Park Centre. The event was hosted by Bill Torrance

of BBC's 'The Beechgrove Garden', and other speakers included Livingston FC manager Jim Leishman, and a number of LDC/Council officials. The award for best local arts organisation went to West Lothian Schools Brass Band, while the best solo artist award went to Mark Boyd. Melanie Meek won the award for best sports individual and West Lothian Cricket Club won the gong for best local sports organisation. Leishman in particular sang the praises both of the winners and of the town itself, and even read one of his famous poems to those present.

Sunday 6th March 1988.

The recently established Livingston branch of the Save the Children Fund issued a public plea for volunteers to knit squares 6" by 6", to be made into blankets measuring 60" by 72". They began a blanket-making competition in Livingston, with entry forms available from Save the Children and from Tiny Togs in The Centre. The charity welcomed donations of single-squares or whole blankets, but asked donators not to use white wool, as white is the colour for mourning in many countries, including in Mozambique, where its blankets were to be sent. The local Safeway store in Deans helped out with the appeal, selling raffle tickets and providing several bottles of Moet and Chandon Champagne as prizes for the raffle and for the blanket competition.

Thursday 7th March 1996.

American company Jabil Circuit announced that it was to axe 85 jobs at its factory in Kirkton Campus, though in the same statement the firm claimed to have already found alternative employment for around half of those who were to be made redundant. They also claimed that the layoffs, blamed on global downturn, had secured the future of the 400 staff who had been kept on.

Friday 8th March 1991.

Census figures were released, containing interesting details about Livingston's demographics/population at the time. Largely due to the expanding Kirkton Campus, the number of people in full-time employment in Livingston had risen from 11,300 in 1982 to just fewer than 23,000 by the time of the Census. This bucked most national trends outwith London and the south-east of England.

Thursday 9th March 1978.

An eleven year-old boy from Craigshill was seriously injured whilst playing on a 'cheese-cutter' in a local play-park. He needed over sixty stitches in the wound and told the local press that he was scared that he might not be able to play football again. He was one of a dozen children injured by the swinging piece of play equipment in the locale in a short space of time. 250 local parents later petitioned LDC and the cheesecutters – now banned completely nationwide- were soon removed. The eleven year-old boy, Roddy Grant, went on to become a reasonably famous professional footballer, best remembered for his time at Perth club, St Johnstone.

Thursday 10th March 1988.

LDC announced that two of its main departments, landscaping and forestry, and maintenance and repairs, were to be merged. However, no timescale was put on the merger and LDC were vague about staffing implications. It was done to streamline operations, and to cut costs, in keeping with a national trend in other local councils.

Wednesday 11th March 1987.

A man from Craigshill appeared in court charged with possessing two pirate copies of the Disney film 'The Jungle Book', and also with possessing pirated videos with intent to supply them to the public. The maximum penalty for video-piracy at the time was £20,000, and the accused was found guilty on both counts. He was fined £250.

Thursday 12th March 1992.

Melville's nightclub in the town held its first 'Armageddon' night, dubbed 'Livingston's New Rock Night.' The party went on from 9pm until 1am and admission was £2. Special drinks offers on the night gave party-goers the chance to buy pints of Dry Blackthorn Cider or Autumn Gold Cider for just 60p each. Not for the first time, cheap drink on a Thursday enticed Livingston's drinkers out for a pre-weekend party at Melville's/Zen/Club Earth.

Tuesday 12th March 1996.

German retailer LIDL opened its brand new state of the art distribution centre at Tailend Farm on the outskirts of Deans. Initially intended to supply 25 stores, it had the capacity to supply four times that number from its vast warehouse. In the beginning there were seventy employees at the site, but the company hoped to grow that number to 120 by the following year. Operations at the 250,000 square-foot facility have increased over the years as the discount chain has grown in the UK. The ground the warehouse is built on was once thought to be unsuitable for construction/industrial use, but these fears have, thus far, proved unfounded.

Monday 13th March 2006.

Supermarket-giant Tesco announced plans to build its new £75m multi-temperature distribution centre at Deans, on the old NEC site. The new warehouse would employ some 1400 staff in warehousing, admin and transport roles. Tesco at the time already employed over 700 staff at a warehouse just across the M8 in Deans Industrial Estate, and most of those staff transferred to the new depot when it opened in 2007. The 400 staff at Tesco's Dundee warehouse, which was to close, were offered the chance to transfer to Livingston, or take redundancy.

Sunday 14th March 2004.

Livingston defeated Hibernian 2-0 in the Scottish League Cup Final at Hampden Park, with goals from Jamie McAllister and Derek Lilley, despite their 5000 fans being outnumbered 8-1 by the Hibs support. Hibs, who had already knocked out both halves of the Old Firm, had been favourites to lift the trophy, but their young and talented but inexperienced team froze on the day, meaning Davie Hay's men were the ones who took the silverware.

Wednesday 15th March 1978.

Angry parents in Dedridge asked LDC to 'properly secure' a building site in the district which was awash with thick, deep mud. One child had already narrowly escaped drowning in the mud on the site, which wasn't fenced off properly. In their defence, the construction company involved, Medway Buildings, pointed out that they already employed a watchman on the site, but that the local children simply ignored his warnings and 'bombarded him with cheek and insults', though Medway did eventually improve the perimeter of the site.

Tuesday 16th March 2004.

A casino-worker from Livingston was jailed for two years after downloading a huge number of child porn images. The first offender, who had been married for 22 years, downloaded 30,000 of the disturbing images on to disks. He was placed on the Sex Offender's Register. He was one of the first internet-perverts in Scotland to be caught by a multi-national sting, having been entrapped after willingly entering credit-card details to the sick, evil website.

Wednesday 17th March 2004.

A seventeen year-old student at West Lothian College became one of the UK's youngest ever National Lottery Jackpot Winners, when she scooped £1.5m in the midweek draw.

Wednesday 18th March 1992.

Some of Lothian's top young musicians performed a concert at The Forum. West Lothian Schools Wind Band and Edinburgh's Secondary Training Orchestra played the 'Grand March' from Aida by Verdi, plus selections from The Yeomen of the Guard. They also performed music by Mozart and Borodin. The concert began at 7.30pm; tickets were £4 for adults, £2 for concessions.

Saturday 19th March 2005.

Frankie and Benny's restaurant and bar chain announced that it was opening a branch in Livingston. The chain's 100th restaurant would open at Almondvale South Retail Park and would become the chain's tenth restaurant in Scotland, following the success of multiple sites in Edinburgh, Glasgow, Aberdeen, Dunfermline and Falkirk. The 132-seater restaurant, which cost £700,000 to develop, was expected to create more than thirty jobs.

Sunday 20th March 1988.

Parents were irate and condemned an organisation as 'irresponsible' for taking fifty-five high-school children from Livingston on a Sunday demonstration against compulsory YTS placements. The protest was organised by The Youth Trade Union Rights Campaign. YTS was a slave-labour scheme in many people's eyes, thought it also helped many of Livingston's youngsters gain vocational training which would stand them in good stead in their working life. It had been created by the Tories in an attempt to mask the true scale of youth unemployment in the UK. The youths' participation in the demonstration caused a public slanging match between the SNP and Labour in the weeks that followed.

Thursday 21st March 1996.

The closure of Littlewoods' huge warehouse in Houston Industrial Estate was announced, with the loss of 81 jobs, as the then huge company tried to cut costs by closing its existing three warehouses across the UK and moving to a single facility in the English Midlands. USDAW pledged to help find work for the axed employees from the three facilities. Littlewoods themselves expressed regret at leaving Livingston in particular, saying that they had enjoyed a good working relationship with the town. MP Robin Cook was a leading voice in attempts to save the doomed warehouse – though there was light at the end of the tunnel for many of its employees, as a huge new Christian Salvesen Warehouse was about to open just across the road from it.

Thursday 22nd March 2007.

Permission was granted for a mobile snack bar to set up in the car park of a major hardware store at the Centre. The food bar was given permission to park at the B&Q retail warehouse at Almondvale, Livingston, for a trial period of a year. The van would displace up to four car parking bays on the site, and the decision by planners to give it the go-ahead was by no means a unanimous one. No objections were received from the public, but some planning officials claimed the snack bar would set an undesirable precedent for similar developments in the town centre, claiming it would 'lower the tone'.

Saturday 23rd March 1991.

A seventeen year-old from Livingston's up-market Deer Park area appeared at Linlithgow Sheriff Court, after he and his friends had caused £3000 worth of damage to Safeway in Carmondean. On the day of the incident some months previously, he was said to have been drinking with friends who he informed that he was going to smash the windows because the shop's staff had been 'hassling him'. All in all, the boy and a large group of his friends had smashed seventeen windows at the shop before running away. As the boy had since reformed himself and taken up an apprenticeship as a joiner and was attending college, he was ordered to do 200 hours community service, and to pay Safeway £500 in compensation.

Monday 24th March 1986.

Malcolm Rifkind MP opened Livingston North Train Station, at Carmondean, the second railway station to open in the town in the space of two years. At first the line that it was built on only travelled from Bathgate to Edinburgh. The current site is very close to the earlier rail-link built in 1849, which Livingston Station's name had derived from. Nowadays, the route passes through Livingston on its way from Edinburgh all the way to the West Coast, and vice-versa, and the area around the station is a vast sprawl of new housing and some new shopping and leisure facilities.

Friday 24th March 1989.

Livingston received perhaps the most important job-related news in its history, with the announcement that SKY had chosen the town for their new operations centre, with all jobs at the Kirkton Campus facility to be given to locals. Initially, the old SMART cards were manufactured there and the company employed 100 people in this task, then a further 150 jobs were created shortly afterwards when part of SKY's customer service call centre was moved there. The rest, as they say, is history. SKY has been perhaps the biggest employer in the town's history, and is so important to Livingston's, and Scotland's economies, that Scotland's First Minister Alex Salmond vowed in 2012 to 'do anything' to keep the company in West Lothian. It also has facilities at two other locations in the UK.

Saturday 25th March 1508.

King James IV spent New-Year - then celebrated in March rather than January- at his wooden hunting lodge at Newyearfield , near where there is now a roundabout , pub and shops. Whilst there with his entourage, he performed the ancient traditional New-Year ceremony of the 'Royal Touch', in which the king placed his hands upon the sick and lame and 'commanded them to be healed', and by many accounts, cured some of them. Prior to the Reformation, people believed that Kings were divinely appointed and possessed healing powers through their touch, or their administering of Holy Water. This practice was continued by Scottish and then British monarchs until William III refused to participate in 1689, when instead he simply gave money to any sick or lame poor people who requested the ceremony.

Monday 25th March 1985.

The New Masonic Hall in Craigshill, Number 1658 Lodge Almondvale, was officially opened and consecrated amid the usual pomp and ceremony.

Thursday 26th March 1992.

Meldrum Primary School in Deans became the first school in West Lothian to officially ban its pupils from playing 'wrestling' in the playground. At the time, WWF was popular in the UK and there were reports in the national press almost daily for a time, of kids injuring themselves trying to copy the moves of actors like Hulk Hogan and The Undertaker. There had been a number of minor injuries at Meldrum because of kids mimicking their wrestling heroes, and angry parents complained to the school after one parent saw kids performing a rather complex move called the 'Tombstone Piledriver' in the playground.

Thursday 27th March 1980.

Local supermarket Presto – which has long since ceased to exist-took out a full page advert in The Livingston Post, giving a great insight into the cost of living at the time. Among its prices advertised were:

Unbranded Sherry 70cl - £1.19
10 x Birds Eye frozen fish fingers – 48p
Bottle of Quash diluting Orange Juice – 26p
White sliced loaf – 20.5p
Tin of Carnation – 17.5p
Can of Coke – 11p
Ambrosia creamed rice – 13p
Tin of Del Monte peach slices – 20.5p
Tin of Heinz Baked Beans – 14.5p
Half-pound of butter – 24p
Tin of John West Salmon – 49p
Packet of Penguin biscuits – 23.5p
Whyte and MacKay Whiskey 70cl - £4.90
Can of Heineken – 19.5p
Can of Whitbread Ale – 20.5p
Can of Tennents Lager – 21p
Can of McEwan's Export – 25p
Pack of 20 Benson and Hedges Cigarettes – 51p
Pack of Regal King-Size Cigarettes – 49p

This was of course when the half-penny coin was still in circulation.

Saturday 28th March 1992.

An 8pm 'till 8am rave night was scheduled to be held in Melville's. Its impressive lineup featured PA's from Praga Khan, New Atlantic and local act Suburban Delay, as well as a host of DJs and MCs. Tickets were £13. Sadly for any would-be party-goers, on the afternoon before the event, police raided the disco in large numbers, with sledgehammers and sniffer-dogs, making a number of arrests, so the event was cancelled. A few days later, Melville's mysteriously burned down.

Thursday 28th March 1996.

West Lothian Trust, in conjunction with 'National Bed-Wetting Day' opened a confidential advice line in Livingston, aimed at tackling the taboos of bed-wetting and bowel problems in the town, and providing confidential advice.

Sunday 29th March 1987.

After eighteen months of reconstruction, Knightsridge Adventure Playground re-opened as Knightsridge Adventure Project. The reconstruction had been necessary after the play-facility had been virtually destroyed by moronic fire-raisers. In addition to the new play structures, it was hoped that the project would also provide after school clubs and evening sessions for teenagers, as well as a proposed multitude of classes and special outings.

Thursday 30th March 1606.

Silver deposits were discovered at Cairnapple, near Bathgate. Though the silver taken from what were three sites was of varying quality, much of it was subsequently used in making the new Scottish Crown Jewels, at the request of King James VI. The jewels containing the silver are now kept beside the historic Stone of Destiny in Edinburgh Castle.

Monday 31st March 1997.

LDC was officially disbanded by Act of Parliament, though it had actually closed and transferred all of its powers to the new local authority, West Lothian Council, at the end of 1996. There had been some opposition to LDC's being disbanded in the preceding decade, but the UK Government was having none of it, though it did 'sweeten' the deal with some £71m to help local infrastructure projects to be expanded and completed on time.

Thursday 31st March 2011.

Disgraced former Livingston MP Jim Devine was jailed for sixteen months at The Old Bailey in London, after being found guilty of making fraudulent expense claims totaling nearly £9000. The bogus claims had been for fictitious cleaning and printing. The disgraced former MP also faced court costs of around £40,000, having pleaded not-guilty to the charges, and was declared bankrupt.

APRIL

Monday 1st April 1996.
Craigshill Social Club was completely destroyed by fire, to the point that there was no option but to demolish the once popular club. The fire was blamed on local teenagers, who it was said had set fire to the club's chairs after breaking in- however, the club had recently been taken over by a firm from East Lothian who planned to turn it into an up-market restaurant, but they had run out of money about a month before the fire, and all building work had stopped. It had been closed for a year before it was burned to the ground.

Saturday 2nd April 1978.
As many as 2000 angry Orangemen from all over Scotland marched through Livingston, in protest against St Columba's Ecumenical Church's ongoing decision to bar them from holding the religious part of their commemorations there, on the grounds that it would be bad for the church's image. The march itself passed off peacefully, ending in a promenade through what was a sun-kissed Howden Park.

Wednesday 2nd April 2008.
A gang of young 'Hoodies' were being hunted after a vandalism spree which saw the tyres slashed on more than 60 vehicles. Police believed that bored youngsters on their Easter holidays were responsible for the attacks. Most of the vehicles were parked around a network of paths linking the Howden, Ladywell, Craigshill and Knightsridge areas of Livingston and Mid Calder, with the damage caused between midnight and 2am.

Monday 3rd April 1978.
A terrified thirteen year-old boy from Knightsridge was 'kidnapped' briefly by a man in a yellow jacket who was driving a van. The man dragged the boy into his van after catching the boy and his friends vandalising a street-lamp beside the road. He then drove

the boy around the town for ten minutes, speaking only once to say 'what the hell do you think you were doing to that light?' before dropping the boy off, completely unharmed, at the exact spot at which he had 'abducted' him from.

Saturday 4th April 1987.

For the second time in four years, Harrysmuir Primary School in Ladywell was gutted by fire. Police believed that the fire was started deliberately, and experts reckoned the damage would cost around £120,000 to repair. No-one was injured in the blaze, which was attended by eight fire-engines from across the region.

Thursday 5th April 2001.

At Linlithgow Sheriff Court, the shocking levels of filth at the Livingston Tandoori were revealed, when the owner admitted nine charges relating to hygiene on the premises and was fined £9000. The court heard that the takeaway, in Main Street, Deans, was visited on three consecutive days by health inspectors in December 1999. Food was lying about where it could be contaminated, the walls, cooking equipment and surfaces were caked with old food, dirt and grease, and the washing-facilities were woefully inadequate. Analysis showed that some food was contaminated with faecal streptococci - human excrement. The premises were also over-run with vermin and insects.

Thursday 6th April 1978.

LDC announced plans to build a new £1m shopping centre in the Carmondean area. Included in the plans were a supermarket, a pub, a petrol station, a library and a health centre. There would be parking capacity for 140 cars as well. All of these facilities are still in use today, though some, most notably the pub and the supermarket, have went under different names since they opened.

Sunday 7th April 1996.

An elderly woman in Craigshill, who asked not to be identified, contacted Livingston Police with concerns about a nasty chain-letter that she had received, which promised her 'lifelong wealth and happiness' if she forwarded the letter to twenty other people, but rather sinisterly, threatened that she would endure bad luck and possibly even bereavement if she chose to ignore it. It also invited her to join an obvious 'pyramid scheme' scam. Police said that hundreds of such identical letters had been received in the town, and they were believed to have originated from a Missionary in Central America, of all places. The transcript of the letter today reads like those tedious 'FWD' emails that most email users are regularly bombarded with, and which are of course, superstitious nonsense.

Friday 8th April 1988.

An American company called Zero Defects spearheaded a triple jobs-boost announced for Livingston this day. Zero Defects were expected to create 100 jobs at their electronics firm, which as their name suggests, had a reputation for reliable products. DHAE, an electronics support company, announced that it too was to set up in Livingston, with the initial creation of twenty jobs. The third part of this boost came from Infotronic Ltd, who made assembly line machinery for factories. LDC welcomed the jobs boost. All three firms had chosen Livingston as they had been unable to recruit suitable workforces south of the border.

Sunday 8th April 2001.

Bigoted morons in Craigshill placed a huge Irish tri-colour on the roof of St Columba's Church hours after Glasgow Celtic had clinched the SPL title. Those responsible were never caught, though the flag was removed that same evening.

Sunday 9th April 2006.

Around forty teenagers from the Ladywell and Knightsridge areas of Livingston clashed in a violent brawl, after arranging to meet at the footbridge dividing the communities. Police officers filmed the fight and were set to use the footage to identify and track down the youths. Three of the youths were arrested at the scene and charged with various offences including assaulting police officers and carrying offensive weapons, in scenes little witnessed in the town for many a year.

Wednesday 10th April 1996.

Members of the public in Livingston were warned to be on their guard – against a ten or eleven year-old bogus charity collector who was operating within the town. The little girl went from door-to-door in Dedridge and claimed that she was collecting for the Dunblane Tragedy Appeal on behalf of the 'Courier. A concerned resident notified the paper, whose staff were quick to announce that they were running no such raffle/collection themselves, and to advise anyone wishing to make a genuine donation to the fund to contact their sister-paper, The Stirling Observer.

Friday 11th April 1997.

A big-footed Scot was left with a problem after thieves stole his size 13 boots. The retired JCB driver from Deans, who had to scour the country every time he needed a new set of footwear, could not believe his bad luck when robbers broke into his allotment shed and made off with his £40 leather boots. The thieves also stole hand tools and broke into other sheds in the Deans area of Livingston. The victim said 'I only have two pairs of shoes - an old pair and these boots. I hope whoever took the boots will realise they are too big to be of any use to anyone else.'

Tuesday 12th April 1966.

Craigshill's first residents, Mr. and Mrs. James Gilchrist and their son Robert, moved in on schedule to 39 Broom Walk. Nearby, the first shop in the new district was opened by former Rangers goalkeeper Billy Ritchie.

Wednesday 12th April 1989.

An updated version of LDC's 'masterplan' report was released, detailing the town's development over the last 25 years. Craigshill, Knightsridge, Deans and Dedridge were described as 'completed', while Ladywell, Howden and Murieston were described as needing 'more work'. The town's excellent transport links via the A71 and M8 were lauded, as were the additions of The Forum, Icelandia and plans for 'Centre Phase Two' and, finally, the new hotel near the centre. Almost 50% of the town's available land was earmarked for new housing, 20% apiece for recreation and industry, and the remainder earmarked for education and healthcare. Also contained in the report was a call for a Roman Catholic High School in Livingston, the main stumbling block being cited as the continued local opposition to the closure of the seriously dilapidated St Mary's Academy in Bathgate. A site in Howden West was already allocated for the proposed RC High School.

Saturday 13th April 2002.
Livingston earned their first ever victory over then-struggling Glasgow Rangers, winning 2-1 at Almondvale thanks to goals from Stuart Lovell and Barry Wilson, after Lorenzo Amoruso had given the Govan side the lead.

Saturday 14th April 2001.
Amid glorious sunshine, Livingston faced Hibernian in a Scottish Cup Semi-Final at Hampden Park, Livingston's first semi-final. The Lions competed well, but went down 0-3 to Hibs, whose scorers were John O'Neill (2) and David Zitelli. The game was watched by 25,000 fans. Asides when Hibs scored, the loudest 'cheers' of the afternoon came when Livingston brought on the ageing striker Darren Jackson, former darling of the Hibs support but now on loan to the Almondvale side from Hearts. Howls of derision from the Hibs end greeted his introduction to the match.

Tuesday 15th April 1651.
A Scottish force of regular cavalry scored a minor victory over English Parliamentarian forces near Livingston. Cromwell's men had been on their way from Edinburgh to Linlithgow when the Scots attacked them. Linlithgow had been occupied by Cromwell's troops after the battle of Dunbar in September the previous year. Scholars disagree over the exact site of this small battle, in which there were few casualties but the invading English were 'put to flight'.

Friday 16th April 1993.
Three masked men with a sawn-off shotgun and a Bowie- knife forced terrified staff at Fernbank Post Office in Ladywell to hand

over a five-figure sum of money. The robbery occurred just before closing time. Police appeared confident of catching the robbers.

Tuesday 17th April 1962.

Livingston formally came into being as a town in its own right, though it would be a year or two before any residents were able to move into any new housing specifically built for the town. However, to all intents and purposes, this date IS Livingston's 'birthday'.

Thursday 17th April 1980.

Craigswood Sports Centre was opened by a local councilor. Livingston's first major public sports facility, when its doors opened it boasted a multi-purpose hall for 5-a-side Football, Badminton and Basketball, two Squash courts, two Pool tables, areas for weightlifting/fitness and a cafeteria. Later, outdoor Tennis courts and Hockey pitches were added, as was a full-length 400m athletics track, and later, a pavilion. Also boasting some full-size outdoor football pitches and training facilities, Craigswood has been Livingston's sporting hub for many a year. It is perhaps best remembered by many for its 'Try-a-sport' clubs in the 1980's, which gave local kids something to do during school holidays.

Wednesday 18th April 1962.

Edinburgh's Scotsman newspaper reported that Livingston would receive its first tenants in 1964. An informative but tongue-in-cheek article also revealed the name of the new-town's council, Livingston Development Corporation. A radio item that evening sarcastically joked that politicians 'must have been up all night thinking up that name'.

Thursday 18th April 2002.

Stunned residents of Livingston's Shiel Walk flats looked out of their windows at lunchtime to find their block surrounded by dozens of police, armed with automatic weapons, sniper rifles and riot shields. Residents were forced to stay indoors as the police burst into what was an empty top- flat. Two Uzis were recovered after the armed police operation, which simultaneously raided a property in

Deans too. Drugs, knives and gas-powered handguns were also seized in the raids. One Shiel Walk resident , who worked back-shift and lived downstairs from one of the raided flats, complained that the police raid had made him late for work, and that his employer hadn't believed the reason for his lateness until details of the raids were broadcasted on the radio later that evening.

Tuesday 19th April 1988.

Sixty-five employees at the Unaform factory in Livingston turned up for work as normal, only to be told that the factory would be closing in a month's time. The company manufactured forming fabrics for the paper and board industry. Its employees, all semi-skilled, were said to be stunned at this news that they said had 'come from nowhere'. The company switched production to a plant in Ramsbottom, near Manchester, and thirty Livingston employees were given the opportunity to switch to the other facility. Unaform, previously known as United Fabrics, had been in Houston Industrial Estate for nineteen years. Their excuse for closure was that the factory was outdated and 'under-utilised', despite having recently spent over £3m on new looms. These new looms were to be moved to the Ramsbottom facility.

Saturday 19th April 2003.

Sixty jobs were been created with the opening of a new nightspot at Livingston Centre. Around £1.8m had been invested in the new Chicago Rock Cafe at the McArthur Glen designer outlet, which opened today. Its owners, Luminar, at the time operated some 300 similar venues in the UK, though they have since went bust, and the aforementioned pub in Livingston has had several owners since.

Wednesday 20th April 1988.

The chairman of Deans Community Council publicly declared Dechmont Law Park as 'a tip, an absolute tip'. The chairman, who lived right beside the park, said that since steps had been installed at the back of her house to make park access easier for the public, several panes of glass had been smashed in her greenhouse, and the area was now strewn with rubbish and stones. In addition to this, huge ruts made by tractors were causing flooding at nearby housing, and children had destroyed most of the new fencing. She raged at LDC and accused them of not being bothered. 'It's like talking to yourself' she said. On the same day, LDC announced multi-million pound plans to further upgrade the park, but also promised to do something about the aforementioned mess too.

Saturday 21st April 2006.
A perverted flasher was being hunted by police after he indecently exposed himself to a 28-year-old woman. She was using the Howden to Ladywell footbridge to cross Cousland Road at about 6pm when the sick pervert struck.

Tuesday 22nd April 1997.
Police and council officials began a full inquiry after a twelve year-old West Lothian boy died under the wheels of a school bus. The tragedy happened in the car park at Inveralmond Community High School in Livingston. The boy was due to catch a bus to his home in Craigshill from the school when he was caught under the wheels of the Lothian Regional Transport bus. Firemen with cutting gear fought in vain to free him.

Thursday 23rd April 1987.
The Dee Corporation opened a 'Gateway' superstore on the site in Livingston Centre that had once housed 'Woolco'. It instantly became the town's largest employer in the retail sector, creating some 400 jobs. It had twenty-two check-outs, including Livingston's first ever check-out specifically designed for wheelchair users. In addition to the store itself, the new unit also contained The Red Balloon Café, which had room for 300 diners, and the site had parking space for 550 cars, a crèche and special trolleys for carrying infants.

Tuesday 24th April 2001.
West Lothian's workers heard the devastating news that over three-thousand jobs were to be axed, as American communications giant Motorola announced that it intended to close its huge Bathgate

factory. Local rumours suggested that the cause may have been persistent theft from the plant, but Motorola confirmed that the closure was part of a global cost-cutting exercise that would see them shed over seven-thousand jobs, in addition to the 22,000 posts that it had already made redundant in the preceding years, blaming 'lack of demand'. The Prime Minister, Tony Blair, tried to intervene, but to no avail, and he described the closure as 'a bitter blow for West Lothian and for Scotland'.

Monday 25th April 1966.
Riverside Primary School in Craigshill was opened, and initially had three, yes, THREE pupils on its register, a figure so silly that it was even derided in the national press, though the school flourished thereafter and remains open today.

Friday 26th April 1996.
Sicko thieves stole a minibus used to transport mentally handicapped children to their playgroup. The £20,000 vehicle, donated by Radio Forth's Help a Child Appeal, was taken from Craigshill, Livingston. It had also been used to take elderly adult members to clubs at Braid House, Howden.

Sunday 27th April 1965.
Livingston Mill Farm's restoration was finally completed, after a five-year project. It is now, of course, a popular place for children to visit with parents, schools and youth clubs. It houses many animals, a soft-play area, and a working mill, among other things.

Friday 28th April 1978.
A terrified eight year-old boy had to be rescued from a dangerous pond in Dedridge, after falling into a deep-pool of what was described as 'sludge' while out looking for tadpoles. He had sank into the mud up to his chin when two local teenagers heard his desperate cries for help and pulled him to safety, saving him from drowning. The boy's mother was obviously relieved, and stated that she was glad that it hadn't been her two year-old daughter who had fallen in, as she would surely have been killed.

Friday 29th April 1988.

A heartless thief ruined days out for the elderly and disabled in Livingston by stealing the fuel distributor from a specially adapted mini-bus. The bus, which had a special hydraulic platform for wheelchairs, had been parked in Heatherbank in Ladywell at the time. When the vehicle wouldn't start that morning, the driver sought professional advice, which revealed that it had indeed been a professional theft. At the time, it was the only such mini-bus in the town available to informal groups, and it was off the road for a week as a result of this sick theft.

Friday 30th April 1976.

An LDC survey revealed the religious make-up of Livingston's school population.

4288 males and 4174 females, plus 47 children whose sex was 'not known', were being schooled in Non-Denominational/Protestant Schools. 1248 males and 1220 females, plus 8 children whose sex was 'unknown' were attending Roman Catholic Schools, despite there still being no Catholic High School in Livingston itself. The same survey revealed that the vast majority of the town's 7940 workers were in the low to medium wage bracket, earning between £10 and £60 per-week.

MAY

Friday 1st May 1987.
Livingston's first ice-rink opened, named 'Icelandia'. It was supposed to have opened at Easter but a delay in delivery of its seats and the 700 pairs of 'for hire' ice-skates meant that it opened slightly behind schedule. It initially proved a popular facility, and in addition to ice-skating, it regularly hosted ice-hockey, curling, ice-discos and a host of private functions in its upstairs suite. It was later opened officially by Robin Cook MP.

Friday 2nd May 1997.
Livingston and the rest of the UK woke up to find that a new era had dawned in British politics, as Labour coasted to a landslide victory over the Tories, gaining their biggest ever majority of 179 seats. Livingston's own Robin Cook MP had easily retained his seat, and became Foreign Secretary, having been shadow foreign secretary in the preceding years.

Monday 3rd May 1999.
A mother and her two children escaped from their West Lothian home after fire raisers caused an explosion. The electricity box outside the house was blown up, causing extensive damage to the front of the end-terraced house in Tweed Drive, Craigshill.

Thursday 3rd May 2007.
In the Scottish Parliamentary Elections, the SNP's Angela Constance won the new seat of Almond Valley, formerly known as Livingston, with a narrow 879 vote lead over her nearest rival, Labour candidate Bristow Muldoon. She was again re-elected to the seat in 2011, this time with a big majority of 5542, amid the SNP's landslide victory which saw them gain an overall majority at Holyrood – an achievement that was intended to be nigh-on impossible when Scotland's new voting system was devised following devolution in 1999. Angela Constance has served as MSP

and has also held several positions within The Scottish Government, and is one of the area's most popular politicians.

Saturday 4th May 1996.
Irish folk-legends 'Athenrye' played a toe-tapping concert at Livingston Forum, to a 450-strong crowd, mostly made up of Celtic supporters. The gig was a great success, despite the fact that the Glasgow side had narrowly lost the league title to rivals Rangers the week before.

Saturday 5th May 2001.
Livingston ended the Division One season with a dull 0-2 defeat at home to Clyde, but had already won the title and been promoted to the SPL thanks mostly to a four-match winning run in the preceding weeks, which had culminated in a 5-0 hammering of Airdrie at Almondvale.

Saturday 6th May 1995.
Meadowbank Thistle played their last ever game at Meadowbank Stadium before their imminent move to Livingston, where they were to be 're-franchised' as Livingston FC. Already relegated to Division Three, they won their last ever home game, beating Stenhousemuir 1-0.

Saturday 7th May 1988.
Livingston ROTARACT held a car-wash at Sidlaw House car-park to raise funds for Multiple Sclerosis research. It cost £1 to get your car washed, and the volunteers were hard at it well until the early evening. ROTARACT was a charity group whose members were all aged between eighteen and twenty-five, it was affiliated to The Rotary Club.

Sunday 8th May 1966.
The first service of Livingston's new Ecumenical Church Confederation, bringing together the town's different Protestant churches under one banner, was held in the youth wing of Riverside Primary School. The Ecumenical group would later splinter, and

later, elements of it were housed in St Columba's Church in Craigshill, which has since been demolished.

Saturday 8th May 1999.

Livingston FC celebrated a fine season by winning 2-1 away to Forfar on the last day of the season, and being crowned Champions of Division Two, having all but secured the title in a thrilling 4-3 victory at Almondvale over nearest rivals Inverness the previous week.

Monday 9th May 1994.

Mitsubishi Electric's fourth Scottish plant, which made air conditioning systems for the European market, was formally opened at Houston Industrial Estate, Livingston. It initially employed 88 people, a figure which was hoped would rise to 200 within two years. Mitsubishi first came to Scotland in 1979, and at the time employed about 1600 people in Livingston, Haddington, and Glenrothes.

Tuesday 10th May 1988.

A Deans mother went to pick up her three month-old daughter, Sadie, for her feed, only to find that the child had went blue around the mouth and had stopped breathing. The mother phoned for an ambulance and gave her daughter the kiss of life, while she waited for the ambulance to arrive. The child was taken to Bangour Hospital but was immediately sent to the Sick Kids in Edinburgh, with a police escort to make sure that she won her heart-rending race-for-life to the Capital. She made it to Sciennes just in time, and her life was saved quite literally at the last minute. The baby made a full recovery, and her mother vowed to help to raise £250 to buy another breathing monitor for the hospital, a vital piece of equipment that had saved her wee daughter's life.

Monday 11th May 1998.

Witnesses were sought by police after a 16-year-old boy from Craigshill, Livingston, was involved in an accident with a car as he crossed the road at the town's Peel roundabout. He was taken, critically ill, to Edinburgh's Western General, where he tragically died.

Saturday 12th May 2001.
Four men stole an enormous Guinness carpet from The Tap Shop pub in Mid Calder, right from under the very noses of staff and customers. The pub later received satirical ransom demands for the carpet by telephone, and even received a phone-call from someone claiming to BE the carpet itself.

Sunday 13th May 1990.

An article in The Sunday Mail revealed that the 'Sky had fallen in' on Bathgate's Trading Standards office – quite literally – as every complaint about the broadcaster which was made in the UK had to be dealt with by the Bathgate office, as SKY's Livingston operations fell under their jurisdiction. Trading Standards said that they had already received twenty-seven complaints in the short time since SKY had opened, and that they expected to be inundated with thousands more.

Saturday 14th May 1994.
Livingston got its first leisure-pool when 'Bubbles' opened down near the Centre. Its name was decided by a competition among local schoolchildren, and 'Bubbles' was the winning suggestion from a local girl. It had waterslides and a gym as well as a pool. Previously, the only places in Livingston where the public could go swimming were the local high-schools.

Tuesday 14th May 1996.
A man found a mysterious object whilst out walking in Murieston, and then put it into his car and drove to the local police station, slamming it onto the counter. Horrified police instantly recognised the item, panicked, and immediately evacuated the station and cordoned it off. It turned out that the object was a WW2 era shell and the bomb-squad was called in. After an hour, the device was declared safe as, thankfully for the five prisoners in the station's cells who hadn't been evacuated along with everyone else, the projectile's

detonator had long since been removed. The man, who it was said genuinely thought he was doing the right thing by handing it in, was nevertheless given a severe 'dressing down' from senior officers at the station. The shell's origins were never discovered.

Friday 15th May 1795.

The stone building that we now know as Howden House was completed, though there are references to the estate in Scottish archives going back as far as the late 16th century. It is impossible to trace the estate's routes back further with any real accuracy because so many church and parish records were destroyed after the Reformation of 1561. The first recorded occupants of the estate were the Douglasses, followed by the Bryces, and the site remains an area of great importance to Livingston today.

Thursday 16th May 1964.

Knightsridge Meeting Rooms were opened by an LDC board member. The buildings were actually two disused shops that had been merged together, and originally hosted an OAP club, a Ladies' club, and a junior drama group. For a time, the rooms were the hub of the Knightsridge community.

Friday 17th May 1996.

Shadow Foreign Secretary and Livingston MP, Robin Cook, officially opened the new £12m Glenmorangie bottling and distribution plant at nearby Broxburn, in a move that was hoped to bring hundreds of jobs to Livingston and the surrounding area. The site had previously been used by United Distillers. Glenmorangie paid nearly £5m for the site, and spent an additional £7m on improving the facility. The move increased Glenmorangie's annual production capacity to a maximum of 24 million bottles per-annum, which were at the time sold in 120 countries.

Friday 18th May 2001.

A father who killed one of his infant daughters and left her twin sister severely brain damaged at their home in Knightsridge was jailed for eleven years at the High Court in Edinburgh. The children had only been home from hospital for ten days. The accused blamed his own violent and abusive childhood for his own actions.

Saturday 19th May 1979.
The town's amateur dramatics group, The Livingston Players, staged a performance of 'Viva Mexico' at Howden Park Centre's Mews Theatre. The play commenced at 7.30pm and tickets cost the princely sum of £1 each.

Friday 19th May 2006.
Police began the hunt for two men in a silver car after two teenage girls narrowly escaped abduction. A sixteen -year-old girl had been walking on Calder Park Road, Mid Calder, at around 2pm when a silver car pulled up. The driver offered her a lift in a forceful manner, and the girl ran off. Then, at about 10pm, a fifteen -year-old girl was standing at the bus stop at Fernbank, Livingston, when a silver car containing the same two men pulled up. The passenger waved to her to approach, then walked briskly towards her and attempted to grab her, but luckily, she escaped.

Friday 20th May 1988.
Scottish popsters Danny Wilson officially opened 'Speakeasy' in Craigshill, an information and counseling centre for people aged between fourteen and twenty-five, involving various organisations, offering everything from advice on benefits and contraception, to confidential personal counseling. Speakeasy went on to be an invaluable resource in Livingston. Danny Wilson were from Dundee and are best remembered for their 80's hit 'Mary's Prayer'. They donated several raffle prizes to Speakeasy.

Saturday 21st May 1988.
Two Mormon Missionaries, Elder and Sister Brown, arrived in Livingston to begin an eighteen-month project, to spread the Gospel of The Church of Jesus Christ of Latter-Day Saints in the town. Elder Brown and three of his sons were qualified dentists, but they didn't come to Livingston to extract teeth. They were said to be 'greatly excited' to have the chance to spread their Gospel in Livingston, and

they were also 'overawed' by Scotland's beautiful countryside. Their Livingston base was at Nelburn Road in Deans. Mormons are a Christian sect who firmly believe that Jesus Christ's second coming happened in America not long after the Crucifixion, and their church was started by their own self-proclaimed prophet, Joseph Smith, in the early 19th century.

Tuesday 22nd May 1866.
The famous explorer David Livingstone (who many people around the world mistakenly think Livingston is named after) laid the foundation stone of the famous Addiewell shale-works. While in the area he stayed with his friend, James Young, at Limefield House near Polbeth. Whilst there, Livingstone planted a Sycamore Tree.

Monday 23rd May 1988.
The shop-keeper who ran the little store in Craigshill's 'Walks' area, and had did so for almost twenty years, complained to the press that he was going to be put out of business, if plans for extending and adding to the shop at the nearby petrol-station were given the go-ahead. The Petrol Station had applied to become a 24-hour convenience store. At the time the BP petrol station operated a 24-hour fuel service and mostly only sold car accessories, but BP wanted to improve their site by adding a full convenience store, new car-wash, and even a restaurant. The main decision at the next council meeting disallowed plans for a Wimpy or other fast-food outlet at the site, but postponed any further decisions until a later date. The garage has long since stopped selling fuel, and the little store in the 'Walks' is still trading – though the garage did eventually become a convenience store in its own right.

Wednesday 24th May 1978.
A new strategy was announced by LDC to 'clean up' the controversial Mall shopping centre in Craigshill. Two uniformed security guards were to be employed after shoppers complained about the Mall's filthy conditions, state of disrepair caused by vandalism, and about the general anti-social behaviour caused by three daily 'invasions' of schoolchildren from the neighbouring

Craigshill High. It was also hoped that the security guards could do something about the small groups of super-lager swilling drunken men who sometimes congregated at The Mall during the day.

Wednesday 25th May 2011.

A twenty-two year-old mother of two young children was brutally stabbed to death by her eighteen year-old boyfriend at their home in Dedridge, after her boyfriend complained that she hadn't made garlic bread to go with their dinner. The victim was stabbed forty times in the frenzied attack. Her family later called for the death penalty to be re-introduced.

Wednesday 26th May 1993.

A little Scots electroplating company which started up in 1990 in West Lothian, today announced a major expansion plan which was likely to see a tripling of the workforce and would hopefully signal a big marketing drive south of the border. Deans Finishing was launched with an initial staff of four in Livingston. They saw a gap in the flourishing manufacturing sector and set up to satisfy the need for an electroplating firm to complement the town's engineering industry. Success had prompted a move from a 4000 square foot unit at Houston Industrial Estate to a new 14,000 square foot facility in Deans Industrial Estate. The move was hoped to help the present staff of 10 to increase to around 32.

Saturday 27th May 1972.

A huge festival was held in Howden Park to celebrate Livingston's tenth birthday, attended by various local dignitaries, and complimented by a battalion of the Royal Scots. Hundreds marched in a colourful cavalcade from Craigshill, through the 'double-tunnels' and on to Howden Park for the day's festivities.

Sunday 28th May 1972.

The former out-buildings at Howden House opened as a theatre and conference centre, the new facility was opened by Andrew Cruikshank MBE, as part of the town's 10th anniversary celebrations.

Sunday 28th May 2002.

Onlookers at Almondvale Stadium witnessed what many would describe as a miracle, after a fourteen-year-old girl, who had been confined to a wheelchair since suffering a brain injury as a small child, got out of her wheelchair and walked onto the pitch when Livingston scored the final goal of their 4-1 demolition of Dunfermline to qualify for the UEFA Cup. So impressed were Livingston's players and staff, that they invited the girl to accompany them on their European adventure the following season.

Monday 29th May 1978.

LDC's annual report predicted that 30,000 new jobs could easily be created in the town by 1990, though the Conservative Party, which took power the next year, and global economic downturn, ultimately rendered these figures greatly over-estimated. Livingston had twelve primary schools, three nursery schools and one secondary school at the time of the report, with a further two secondary schools at Deans and Ladywell currently under development. The report also welcomed the near completion of a championship standard golf course and club-house at Knightsridge, or as we now know it, Deer Park.

Thursday 30th May 1996.

The unfortunately named 'Schindlers Lifts' elevator manufacturers announced that their recent takeover could see dozens more jobs created at its Livingston factory. In the same year, the company changed its name to simply 'Schindlers', as their previous name had in recent years become the subject of much mirth and even offence due to its similarity to the name of a recent Hollywood blockbuster movie about the Holocaust , named 'Schindler's List.'

Tuesday 31st May 1988.

The owners of Brucefield Farm finally received permission from LDC to convert some of their buildings into a licensed bar and a restaurant. A similar application by the farm's previous owners had been given such permission in 1982 but they had never acted on it, and the time period for that development had since lapsed. Future proposals also included a 24-space car-park, and a possible guest-house in one of the farm's other out-buildings.

JUNE

Monday 1st June 1997.
A woman died in a house fire while her family called in vain for her to escape. She collapsed in an upstairs bedroom at her home in Whinbank, Ladywell, as her son and daughter encouraged her to get out. The fire was thought to have been started by a chip pan.

Friday 2nd June 1978.
The press reported that the number of women looking for work in Livingston was continuing to rise. Figures given to the press by the Job Centre showed that 587 females were looking for work, a 16% increase on the previous month. The figures also showed a minor improvement in local jobless figures though, with 1314 men and women currently looking for work, an improvement of 43 on the previous month. These figures included Livingston, Bathgate, West Calder and Broxburn. At the time, the area was 4th in the Scottish 'Jobless table', with an out-of-work rate of 8.6%.

Tuesday 2nd June 1987.
A £500,000 leisure funding deal for Livingston was announced. It gave West Lothian Youth Theatre a permanent home in Craigshill and was also intended to turn Livingston South into a major sporting area.

Friday 3rd June 1978.
Tragedy struck a Livingston family for the second time in twelve months as their house was destroyed by fire in the early hours of the morning. The family dog suffocated in the inferno. Seven months previously, the family had suffered an even worse tragedy, as their infant child had died of cot-death.

Saturday 4th June 1989.
Livingston-born Paul Dickov was saint turned sinner in the Under 16's World Cup Final at Hampden Park, as he scored in the match

which finished 2-2 after extra-time, but went on to miss in the deciding penalty shoot-out that Scotland lost against what was a suspiciously over-age looking Saudi Arabia side. The 'under 16' Saudi team were later spotted out celebrating their win in Glasgow's nightclubs. Dickov though, like the rest of the Scotland team, was still a hero to the people of Scotland.

Wednesday 5th June 1985.

Zhao Ziyang, Premier of the Chinese Peoples Republic, visited Ferranti Infographics in Brucefield Industrial Estate. He was welcomed by pupils of Bellsquarry Primary School, and arrived under heavy police guard. Later, his trip to Livingston saw him accused of 'promoting Capitalism' when he went home to China, and that, coupled with his outspoken opinions on the disgraceful Tiananmen Square massacre of 1989, eventually saw him spend fifteen years under close house-arrest for being an 'enemy of the people'.

Saturday 6th June 1981.

In another of Livingston's most famous incidents, a full-scale riot broke out after police tried to disperse a house-party in Craigshill's Brisbane Street, at which SEVENTY people had been in attendance. Dubbed 'The night the punks turned ugly' by the local press, once out in the street, the Punks allegedly chanted 'There's only one Yorkshire Ripper' to the police. Police made some arrests but were showered with assorted missiles by the mob, including cans, bottles, and planks of wood torn from nearby fences. The Punks themselves gave a very different account, claiming that only fifty people had been at the house-party, and that they had only been shouting at and swearing at the police, not attacking them. Eight of the party-goers were charged with various public order offences, though they claimed to themselves have been victims of violence at the hands of the police, including sustained truncheon attacks by one officer after they had been arrested and taken to the police station in Elm Grove. There were several inconsistencies in both 'sides' stories, and four of the punks made official complaints about one of the police officers.

Friday 7th June 1811.

James Young Simpson was born near Bathgate. He studied Midwifery and Medicine at Edinburgh University. He is best known for his discovery of Chloroform, which has revolutionised surgery and pain relief all over the world. He first tested the substance on his dinner party guests one evening, watching them all pass-out one by one, though thankfully, they all survived being his 'Guinea Pigs', completely unharmed.

Saturday 7th June 1851.

The red sandstone building of Knightsridge House was completed, near where the much older original mansion with the same name was located. It gives its name to a residential district of Livingston. The name 'Knightsridge' was derived from the fact that The Knights of St John once owned the land and had their headquarters at nearby Torphicen. The Knights of St John are best remembered for their heroic defence of Malta from The Ottoman Turk attack in 1565, as The Turks tried to capitalise on Europe's temporary weakness and disunity caused by The Reformation.

Wednesday 8th June 1650.

English Parliamentary Soldiers looted Livingston Kirk and virtually razed it to the ground, during Cromwell's invasion of Scotland.

Monday 9th June 2003.

A huge new superstore and retail warehouse was on the cards for Livingston, following a multi-million pound land deal with West Lothian Council. Property chiefs at the local authority today recommended that a £27m bid by development firm Deansway Developments for a sixteen-acre council-owned site at Dedridge North had been accepted. Many local residents in Dedridge opposed the plans, as they wanted affordable housing to be built on the site instead. The site now houses B&Q, Morrisons and Sainsbury's.

Friday 10th June 1904.

Livingston's first 'Co-op' store opened, albeit in what was then known simply as Livingston Station, now Deans. In its first year of trading, it acquired 100 members, and turned over some £3030.

Thursday 11th June 1987.

Robin Cook thrashed all of his opponents to reclaim his Livingston seat in the General Election, winning a majority of almost 12,000, confirming Livingston's status as a safe Labour seat. The SNP finished last in Livingston, beaten even by the almost universally despised Tories. It was a bright spot on an otherwise dark night for Labour, who lost the election to Thatcher's Tories, Labour's leader Neil Kinnock having been preoccupied with 'sorting out' the hard-left in his own party in the run up to the election. In Livingston, The Alliance Party came second.

Thursday 12th June 1315.

Not long after securing his kingship, King Robert Bruce gifted Bathgate Castle to the High Steward, Lord Walter, upon his marriage to Bruce's daughter, Princess Marjorie. Walter died in 1328, as the founder of what would become The Royal House of Stewart, who would be Scotland's Kings and Queens in one shape or form until Queen Anne's death in 1714 – though the direct Stuart line was deposed by the Dutch Invasion of 1688.

Monday 12th June 1843.

Murieston Castle was demolished as locals stole all of its stones to build cottages for themselves. Curiously, the first reliable reference to the structure and its arrow loopholes was made in 1790, centuries after the castle or 'peel' had fallen out of use. This structure should not be confused with Livingston Peel, which was situated where Livingston Village stands today.

Tuesday 12th June 1984.

The Inferno Scooter Club was formed and ran until 1987. Named after the Northern Soul record label, it was made up of mods, scooter boys and the 'Livi Punks'. Later, it merged with the still- running

65

'Coyotes' in Uphall. Many ex-members still ride Vespas and Lambrettas around Livingston to this day.

Thursday 13th June 1996.

West Lothian Council announced that over 100 foster-carers in the area were to be quizzed as to whether or not they had any firearms in the house. This of course came in the wake of the shootings in Dunblane that year, and the actions of sicko Thomas Hamilton had understandably created nationwide anti-firearm hysteria. At the time, whether or not prospective foster or carer families possessed firearms was not a consideration when judging their suitability for their role, though they were considered 'unsuitable' to care for anyone if they owned a dangerous dog like a Pit-Bull or a Rottweiler. The issue of carers possessing firearms had been brought to light when one such carer admitted at a meeting that he kept shotguns in his house, as he lived in the countryside. In the end, action against the ownership of firearms was taken at UK Government level, rendering this local debate redundant.

Tuesday 14th June 1977.

Craigshill Job Centre was broken into by thieves, who got away with the princely sum of £32. Police appealed for information. During the robbery, the job-centre was also vandalised.

Friday 15th June 1973.

LDC's report to the Secretary of State for Scotland, Gordon Campbell, revealed that Howden Park Centre being opened for public use had proved a master-stroke in the town's favour. Twenty-four conferences has been held there, including four major British Leyland Conferences and a reception for Britain's Everest Team, held by Paterson's Shortbread . It had also hosted sixteen plays, concerts and pantomimes, as well as seven events simply listed as 'other'. The same report also made some important announcements regarding recreation in the town. Two major-contracts were announced for projects that would see the following facilities created in Livingston.

Seven much-needed play-parks in Craigshill.

A cadet hut for army cadets, at the top of Craigshill, funded by the Duke of Edinburgh Award Scheme/Princes' Trust.

Three Tennis-Courts in Craigshill.

An accessible country-park beside the River Almond. (Which is now Almondell Country Park.)

Two ash football pitches in Craigshill.

A pavilion at Craigpark.

A small golf-course at the bottom of Howden.

LDC also announced plans for a number of new licensed premises within the town and the regional centre, in addition to Livingston's newest pub, The Stirrup Stane. Plans were also unveiled for a large hotel in the town, but that project was mothballed for a time.

Thursday 15th June 1978.

Local press ran a feature about a Livingston man who had been going around Livingston collecting, of all things, discarded ring-pulls. In the six months since he had started collecting, he had acquired over 7000 ring-pulls. The man, from Craigshill, said that he hoped to find some sort of organisation to buy the ring-pulls from him, so that he could donate the money to Cancer Research. He often collected the ring-pulls in bulk from places like Woolco, and was aided in his collecting by friends and neighbours.

Friday 16th June 1978.

Livingston United, so long considered the 'country cousins' of Scottish junior football, announced plans to move into a new stadium in the town's Deans area. The stadium, it was thought, would cost £100,000 to build, finally giving the team a permanent home. That stadium is, of course, Station Park.

Friday 17th June 1983.

LDC released a paper containing its updated development profile. It was hoped that one day, as many as 100,000 people would live in Livingston. For the first time, it was recognised officially that the style of housing in Livingston needed to change, as many second-generation 'Livingstonians' sought places to live – in other words, more flats and pensioners' houses were needed, rather than big family homes. The paper called for the building of these homes to be split equally between the public and private sectors, and Livingston was hailed as having enjoyed unprecedented prosperity during the 1970's, despite the recession and changing world economy. The reasons for Livingston's success, in addition to its people, were listed as:

Its excellent transport links.

Central Government assistance.

EEC/EU assistance.

Lack of 'red tape', which allowed new businesses to set up easily within the town.

The paper also stated that there had only been around 600 jobs per year created in the town in the last few years, well below the target of 1000, but also claimed that as many as 1300 new jobs per year would have been created had it not been for Thatcher's ideologically driven cuts in public spending, cuts which the vast majority of Scots did not even vote for. The paper ended with a stark warning – The town was over-reliant on immigrant industry, i.e. foreign companies, for too many of its jobs. 82% of jobs in the town at the time relied on 'immigrant industry.'

Sunday 18th June 1978.

A huge celebration party was held in The Tower in Craigshill, as the pub's football team beat Cameron Club 2-1 to clinch the Sunday league title. The team had also won the Ashdon and Brown cup that season. The Tower's team was truly a juggernaut that season, and in total they scored 183 goals while only conceding 27 in all competitions. Mr. Roy, who managed the pub, filled the trophy with Champagne, and the players all took a well-deserved swig from the trophy that they had brought home to Craigshill.

Friday 18th June 2004.

The distraught family of a six-year-old boy faced an agonising wait to see if he had contracted a deadly disease after stabbing himself with a dirty syringe. The youngster had picked up the needle - which was believed to have been dropped by a drug user - after spotting it while hunting for treasure in woods beside Harrysmuir Primary School in Ladywell, but as he ran towards a group of friends, he tripped and accidentally stabbed himself in the chest.

Thursday 19th June 1679.

James, Duke of Monmouth, illegitimate son of King Charles II, arrived in Blackburn, West Lothian, at the head of two troops of cavalry, where he raised a local militia unit to bolster the King's Army before its victory over the forces of a radical, intolerant but fiercely patriotic, Scots-Presbyterian Taliban-style sect known as The Covenanters, at Bothwell Brig, three days later.

Friday 19th June 1992.

Craigshill High School closed its doors for the last time, after being shut-down in the latest round of Tory cuts. In its last term, it had less than 300 students on its rolls. The school had opened in 1969 with just 120 pupils and had cost around £1m to build. At its peak, Craigshill High had 1487 pupils and 100 teachers. After its closure, most of its students moved to Inveralmond High School in Ladywell.

Tuesday 20th June 2006.

A twenty-nine year-old man from Livingston was arrested, accused of fraudulently obtaining more than £7 million from banks in the City of London after pretending to be a banker. One of the six charges facing the man was for obtaining £600,000 from the Royal Bank of Scotland in a single money transfer, by falsely representing that he was employed by Syrian Airlines. By far the worst fraud ever committed by a Livingstonian.

Friday 21st June 1996.

The BBC's 'Beechgrove Garden Hit-Squad' faced their biggest challenge yet, though this time their green-fingers would be used for something a little bit different. The 'dynamic-duo' joined local councilors in a sponsored abseil down Sidlaw House, in an event supervised by the local army cadet training team. In total, 150 people participated in the charity event to raise £10,000 in one day for St

John's Hospital's MacMillan Centre. MacMillan nurses and staff participated in the abseil, as did teams from LDC, Renault, West Lothian College, Mitsubishi and the Post Office.

Saturday 22nd June 1985.
A gang-fight raged in Howden Park under the sweltering summer sun, as around forty young men and teenagers knocked lumps out of each other. One group is said to have been made up of a mix of some members of a Craigshill gang named after a famous American soccer team, supplemented by Celtic and Hibernian fans from the town, while the other group was mostly made up of fans of Rangers and Hearts, also from the town. Records indicate that no-one was seriously injured and that there were no arrests, as the combatants fled the scene when police arrived.

Monday 23rd June 1969.
Deans Primary School was opened in Mid Street, the first school opened in Livingston by West Lothian Education Authority, with an original roll of 300 pupils. Another school had already been opened in Livingston by Midlothian Council three years earlier, at Riverside.

Monday 24th June 1963.
LDC's first annual report to The Secretary of State for Scotland about the town was submitted. It re-affirmed the two basic aims of Livingston's creation – to solve housing shortages, and to economically revitalise a central belt which had been over reliant on mining and other 'outdated' industries, by creating, it was hoped, 1,000 new jobs per year. Plans were also included in the report for Livingston's Coat-of Arms, which it was proposed should contain the Heraldry emblems of De Leving and Roseberry, as well as a representation of the River Almond. The town's first complete 'balance sheet' was also contained in the report, and makes interesting reading now, even though it was pre-decimilisation.
Total budget - £41, 754
Works contracts - £1600
Uncertified work - £145
Retention - £5

Government departments and creditors owed - £4506
Local Authority expenses - £368
'Advance' payments - £160
Other creditors - £5502
Repairs and maintenance - £45
Emergency repairs £26
LDC was owed £180 by other public bodies and £172 by individuals, as well as £380 by private companies.

Saturday 25th June 1977.
The Lanthorn community centre was opened by the Secretary of State for Scotland, in Dedridge. Remembered by many for the odd concrete sheep that sat outside, it has fulfilled a number of roles for the local community over the years. The Queen visited it in 1978, planting a tree to commemorate the occasion.

Saturday 25th June 1994.
Hundreds of clubbers danced the night away at Awesome 101's event 'Clash of the Titans' at The Bunker in East Calder. The line-up included Q-Tex, N-Joi, Tom Wilson, Mikey B, Bass Generator, Chubb Kray and a host of other stars of the rave scene. The event was preceded by an early-evening gig for under 18's, headlined by Q-Tex and N-Joi.

Saturday 26th June 2010.
A 23 year-old mother of three small children was killed in a tragic house-fire in Ambrose Rise, Dedridge. The blaze was attended by Fire Crews from Livingston and West Calder, such was its severity. Dozens of bunches of flowers were left as tributes near the scene of the fire, and a benefit night at Club Earth was arranged to raise money for the victim's children.

Friday 27th June 1986.
The last 2000 workers were made redundant in a move that would signal the end of the British Leyland Plant at Bathgate, in what was a huge blow to the local economy. Inspired by the great Trade-Unionist James Larkin, the plant's valiant workers had tried almost

everything to reverse the decision to close the facility, including occupying it. The closure of the huge plant was lamented in The Proclaimers' first big-hit 'Letter from America' with the simple lyric 'Bathgate no more'.

Tuesday 28th June 1988.

After a house fire in Livingston in which a little girl had died, and a recent spate of domestic blazes throughout West Lothian, LDC announced that it was to install smoke-detectors in each of its 9300 homes, and would also send all of its tenants a leaflet about fire safety and prevention. This was another fine example of Livingston pioneering something that would later become standard operating procedure for councils across the UK, and which was later underpinned by Westminster regulation.

Friday 29th June 1979.

Thousands of dead fish were discovered floating on Murieston Water by a dog walker. The fish, mostly Brown Trout, had died of Chlorine Poisoning and the ghastly spectacle of their lifeless carcasses covered three-quarters of a mile of the watercourse. It was established that the deaths had been caused by some 14,000 gallons of Industrial Chloride being dumped in the water about one mile away from the scene. Fishing was, of course, suspended until stocks could be replenished, but it was not thought that any permanent damage would befall the watercourse as a result of the pollution.

Tuesday 29th June 2004.

A teenager from West Lothian became the first person in Scotland to be served an Anti-Social Behaviour Order for stalking, after allegedly targeting a girl and her family. The seventeen year old youth was banned from Livingston's Centre, and from three streets around the home of his alleged victim and her family. The ban followed a campaign of harassment said to have been carried out on the girl and her family in the Murieston area of the town. The youth was understood to have been going out with the girl until the relationship ended some ten months previously. The harassment was alleged to have included following the parents to work and shouting verbal abuse and assaulting them.

Tuesday 30th June 1987.

The Queen again visited Livingston, as part of the town's 25th birthday celebrations. She went on a brief walkabout, then she and her extensive entourage officially opened Mill Farm.

Friday 30th June 1995.

Abel Eastern Foods in Houston Industrial Estate was burned to the ground in a ferocious blaze, the day after its buildings insurance policy had expired. The company had been building an extension and had been operating in Livingston for some eight years. The company, which made Indian food, was unable to continue trading, and 300 people lost their jobs as a result.

JULY

Sunday 1ˢᵗ July 2007.

A bogus 'war-veteran' from Livingston, who had never been in the army, took part in a parade in Edinburgh wearing medals he had bought on eBay. He marched with veterans of the 3rd Battalion of the Parachute Regiment, who had served in the Falklands twenty-five years previously. The bus-driver from Livingston later admitted he should never have taken part in the commemorative service, and said he was ashamed of having marched with genuine veterans from the conflict. He also apologised for any offence that his actions may have caused.

Friday 2ⁿᵈ July 2010.

A gambling addict from Carmondean, who claimed Job Seeker's Allowance while he was holding down three jobs, appeared for sentencing at Livingston Sheriff Court. The fifty-eight year old had been 'on the fiddle' for seven years, but his luck had ran out when a 'grass' alerted the Department of Work and Pensions, telling them he was working at Celtic Park in Glasgow. He was jailed for a year after earlier admitting to claiming £40,000 in Jobseekers Allowance.

Wednesday 3ʳᵈ July 1314.

The Battle of Livingston Peel was fought, after a short siege. Livingston Peel – a small fortress believed to have been located near present-day Livingston Village- had been the private property of Sir Archibald Livingston, a pro-English Scot who was steadfast in his support of the English cause against both the Balliol and the Bruce parties. The Peel was a timber fort with a palisade and had a garrison of ten men-at-arms, including Sir Archibald himself, and ten archers, most, if not all, of whom were Scots. Its garrison was also bolstered by a few dozen fugitives from the English army that had recently been destroyed at Bannockburn. It is not clear whether Livingston Peel was constructed before or immediately after the invasion of 1296. It fell to the Scots after this battle and was destroyed by King Robert Bruce in line with his general policy of destroying captured fortifications. The Pro-English garrison were slaughtered by the Scots after they had stormed the fort, only Livingston himself was spared. It's important to remember that Scots from Lothian at that time often sided with England, not because of great loyalty to England, but because invading English armies usually travelled through West Lothian on their way to fight Scots forces in the Stirling area. It was rare for Scots to attack the invading English before they reached the Stirling area.

Tuesday 4th July 1961.
The Secretary of State for Scotland officially announced to the Scottish Grand Committee that a site 'in or near The Calders' to the west of the Capital was to be the location of the next new-town. Things, of course, would have been very different for us all if the other mooted location, near Lugton in Ayrshire, had been chosen instead.

Monday 4th July 1983.
The Queen, amid much pomp and ceremony, officially opened the NEC Semi-conductor plant at Deans in Livingston, though it had been open for a while by then. The plant cost some £40m to construct and provided many much-needed jobs in the town for almost twenty years.

Wednesday 5th July 1978.
The Queen visited Livingston, going for a walkabout in the town with Reverend McLaren, and was greeted by excited, curious crowds wherever she went. She also visited several locations in Dedridge.

Thursday 5th July 1979.
Twenty Piglets, valued at around £400 in total, were stolen from a Piggery near Livingston. It was the second time in a year that the Piggery had been targeted by thieves, and the facility's owners were sure that they would never see their pigs again, despite offering a generous reward. Defiant, they also said that they expected to hear the pitter-patter of tiny trotters soon, as more piglets were born.

Monday 6th July 2009.

Local vandals caused thousands of pounds worth of damage in a wrecking spree at a bowling club, pouring paint on the green and smashing their way into the clubhouse. The vandals attacked Deans Bowling Club in Livingston, before they were forced to flee after triggering the main building's noisy alarm.

Friday 7th July 2006.

Some teenagers from Livingston were praised by police after saving a pensioner's life, after the seventy-seven year-old man, who had dementia, went missing and fell into a stream. The youths were playing in Murieston woods when they heard a cry for help and helped the elderly man to safety. Police issued a statement commending the boys' courage, saying 'It's fantastic to see boys of this age going out of their way to stop and help those in need'.

Monday 8th July 1985.

Scottish Youth Theatre began a five-week programme of workshops, classes and rehearsals at Howden Park Centre as part of their annual summer festival. Anyone between the ages of twelve and twenty-one was welcome to participate in the events, which covered most aspects of the performing arts. Thus began Livingston's long and successful affiliation with Youth Theatre.

Thursday 9th July 1987.

Residents in the Gorsebank and Forestbank areas of Ladywell appeared in the 'Courier, expressing their deep concern about the lack of a suitable perimeter fence between their adjacent play-park and the town's busy dual-carriageway. In the preceding year a twelve year-old child and a resident's dog had been killed on the busy road, while there had also been numerous near-misses. LDC later pledged to fix the problem, but one spokesman said that it was human nature to take shortcuts, so he could never see the problem of people trying to walk across the busy road disappearing altogether.

Tuesday 10th July 1979.

Two huge explosions ripped through parts of the new sports centre at Craigswood, causing extensive damage but thankfully, not injuring anyone. People living up to a mile away from the blast reported that it shook their windows. The Fire Brigade and Police said that the explosions had occurred because the roof had recently been tarred, and the tar had overheated in the summer sun, causing gas cylinders to explode. Locals described the noise as sounding 'like a bomb had went off'. 15,000 gallons of water were used to extinguish the resulting fire as police formed a cordon to keep curious residents away from the scene.

Monday 11th July 1988.

An eighteen year-old man from Dedridge went to see his local councilor after losing his job at what was then Livingston's Hilton Hotel. That in itself may sound unremarkable, but the young man had lost his job because of his new £14 haircut! The excuse given by his employers was that 'he had been unwilling and unable to comply with the company's hair requirements, as his heavily gelled hair could be deemed disrespectful to their customers'. The man claimed that he had had the haircut in a bid to look smarter at work. The Hilton refused to comment any further on the matter.

Thursday 12th July 1990.

The Queen opened the stunning new, state of the art, St John's Hospital in Livingston, a facility built to replace the ageing and no longer fit-for-purpose Bangour Hospital at nearby Dechmont. The hospital's opening prepared West Lothian's health services for the challenges posed by Livingston's growing population, and as well as general medicine and 'Accident and Emergency' services, also offered a wide range of acute services that had previously only been available in nearby Edinburgh. Some services at the hospital have been moved back to Edinburgh in recent years because of spending cuts, much to the concern of the local populace.

Friday 13th July 1979.

It certainly was an unlucky Friday for fourteen children from Deans Youth Club as they had to be sent home from an outdoor centre in Dumfries that they had been supposed to stay at for the weekend. Filthy toilets, dirty blankets, spider infested dormitories, overflowing bins and a revolting, nauseating smell were among the many complaints of child and adult alike, so they simply came home. The group's leaders expressed their disappointment as they had stayed at the same place a year previously, and had experienced none of these problems on that occasion.

Saturday 13th July 1982.

A sectarian orange walk in Craigshill was targeted by local mischief makers who were sick of their weekend peace being disturbed by such marches and by some of the morons who used to follow the 'walk around. The flute band had bricks, stones, eggs and bottles of urine thrown at it , mostly targeted at the band's bass-drummer and baton twirler, and received a verbal roasting from Craigshill people of many backgrounds. The eggs thrown had been out of date eggs, 'liberated' from the back of the Co-op, where they had been due to be thrown in the skip. The band's members had little luck in chasing the mischief makers, who cunningly used the area's underpasses for cover, and then escaped on mopeds or bicycles.

Tuesday 14th July 1981.

The old Livingston Police Station, headquarters of what was at the time 'F' Division of Lothian and Borders Police, was opened by a local council convenor.

Friday 15th July 1988.

Only minutes after discovering what it actually was, LDC's board members discussed whether or not to 'wave' goodbye to one of the town's most famous pieces of public sculpture. The piece in question was the silver column with a squiggle on top that was located on the

Dedridge-Burn greenway, between the old multi-storey car park and the hotel. At the time, the sculpture was the subject of numerous complaints as it was absolutely caked in bird droppings, but LDC gave it a stay of execution, for the time being.

Friday 16th July 1995.

An animal cruelty officer found eight poodles living in squalid conditions at the home of two dog breeders in Deans, in conditions described as 'callous and filthy'. The breeders were subsequently fined £200 each. One of the breeders had already been banned from keeping dogs for ten years, after a previous offence.

Sunday 17th July 1988.

The SNP's Kenny MacAskill told a protest meeting in Livingston that only a campaign of non-payment would put an end to the Tories' unpopular Poll Tax. He told those assembled that new Tory legislation meant that even those who did not register to pay would still receive a bill, and that, therefore, not registering for it was a futile act in trying to defeat the tax. The only way to get rid of the unfair tax was a campaign of non-payment. He was to be proved right, and the tax was scrapped shortly after being introduced in the UK, Scotland having been used as a testing ground for it in its first year.

Wednesday 18th July 2001.

West Lothian College opened in the middle of Livingston, having moved from its previous run-down location in Bathgate. It cost £18.1m to build and originally employed some 240 people. Initially, only seven courses were available to students. Over 10,000 students attended it in its first year alone.

Tuesday 19th July 2005.

It was announced that more than 2000 people had applied for work at a new warehouse, which was set to open in the autumn. B&Q bosses revealed there had been huge interest in the 250 jobs available at the firm's new 120,000 square foot warehouse in Livingston. General manager Grant Anderson said 'We've had an amazing response to our recruitment campaign, with more than 2000 people inquiring about the 250 vacancies.'

Friday 20th July 1984.
A joint-study by the somewhat bizarre partnership of the NUM and The Royal Geographical Society was concluded. Its results showed conclusively that there was enough coal under West Lothian alone to sustain mining for about 500 years.

Saturday 21st July 1984.
The Bankton House Hotel opened in the town's Murieston area. Built in 1812 as a country mansion, by the mid 1900's it had fallen into dereliction and disrepair. Many local children believed the building to be haunted, and until a local businessman converted it into a bar/hotel, it was known locally simply as 'The Haunted House'. Hanging around it and another similar building nearby at night became a common 'dare' among local youngsters.

Friday 22nd July 1988.
There was great news for Craigshill's peckish residents, when Craigsfarm Café re-opened after being closed for a time for refurbishment. The refurbishment gave the popular café a more 90's feel, yet the staff and friendly service ensured that it lost little of its original charm. The refurbishment had been the first stage of a wider renovation of Craigsfarm.

Saturday 23rd July 1966.
Howden House underwent another transformation as it was officially opened as a community centre for the first time. Initially it contained the YWCA and the Citizens' Advice Bureau. One of the most famous old buildings in the town, its grounds were to play host to dozens of gala-days and events over the years, and are now known simply as 'Howden Park' by locals. Its future is currently unclear.

Friday 24th July 2009.
After numerous warnings, The Court of Session in Edinburgh finally placed Livingston FC into administration following its

financial disputes with several creditors, most notably, and ironically, West Lothian Council. The club was forced to form a 'Newco' and had to start from scratch in Division Three.

Monday 25th July 1988.

A two-minute visit to a local shop ended in heartbreak for a Livingston boy, as his new skateboard was stolen. The boy said that 'all of the fun had been taken out of his school holidays'. He had bought the skateboard after saving up his 75p per-week pocket money for a time until he had the £12 he needed to buy the skateboard. The theft, at Dedridge Village Store, happened when the boy and his dad went into the shop for two minutes, leaving the skateboard outside, as per the instructions in the shop window, where it was then stolen, despite the fact it was being 'guarded' by the family dog. The dog however, it was said, was 'too friendly' and didn't stop the thief. A subsequent search of the area by the boy's father found no sign of the skateboard, but the boy vowed to save up and buy another one as soon as he could.

Thursday 26th July 1979.

Largely thanks to their union, NALGO, LDC staff were awarded bumper pay-rises, some worth as much as £3000 a year. The increases in wages ranged from 9% for white-collar workers, to up to 45% for those employees already on the higher salary scales.

Wednesday 27th July 1977.

For the first time since the town's inception, a sizeable number of households surveyed by the LDC about their religious background gave the answers 'Don't know' or 'Atheist'. The survey's results were.

Roman Catholic – 18.2%
Church of Scotland – 58.3%
'Other' Protestant - 8.4%
Don't Know/Atheist – 14.1%
Refused to answer – 1%

Saturday 28th July 2001.

Livingston played their first ever SPL match, beating Hearts 2-1 at Almondvale, in what would be a remarkable season for the club, who finished third in the SPL and qualified for the UEFA Cup.

Monday 29th July 1996.

A teenager, high on sherry and Temazepam when he bludgeoned an 81-year-old woman over the head as she lay helpless on the floor of her Knightsridge home, was sentenced to eight years' detention at the High Court in Edinburgh. The woman had woken to find the youth standing at the end of her bed, demanding money. The doctor who treated her took the view that, given the force that was used, she was fortunate not to be more seriously injured as at least one of the blows had been delivered with 'extreme force'.

Wednesday 30th July 2003.

The burns unit at St John's Hospital was closed for admissions after a scare involving the superbug MRSA. The entire unit had to be deep-cleansed for the second time in three months. The bug, SMRSA 155, was brought into the unit by a Livingston-born patient who was transferred from St James' Hospital in Dublin after an assault and arson attack.

Wednesday 31st July 2002.

Freakish heavy thunderstorms ravaged Scotland, with West Lothian in particular having to endure a genuine 'Baptist's Downpour'. The M8 was closed for a time, and fire engines had to pump water away from the village of Uphall Station, where several feet of water was threatening more than thirty homes.

AUGUST

Monday 1st August 1988.

The first of a newly-refurbished development of thirty-one private flats went on sale in Craigshill. The flats, in Forth Drive, were said to be amply sized, with two bedrooms, living room and kitchen. The flats initially cost £18,000 to buy and had been ex-LDC flats, refurbished by Cruden Homes. There was a surprise in store for any would-be buyers. The flats had electric white-meter heating, smoke detectors, an improved entry-door system, mirrored wardrobe doors in the bedrooms and luxury kitchen units. Some of the flats even had window-boxes for growing plants in.

Tuesday 2nd August 1988.

Nine deadly fibreglass bows and a considerable amount of arrows were stolen when the sports barn at Crofthead Farm was broken into. The bows and arrows, property of the Dedridge Archers Club, were said by a club official to be 'extremely dangerous and easily capable of going straight through a human being' as they fired arrows at 200 feet per second. The club, which did a lot of charity work in the town, was said to be 'sickened' by the theft. The thieves gained entry to the premises using bolt-cutters, which indicated that it had been an organised theft, but they also set fire to some other archery equipment that couldn't be carried away. In total, the theft cost the archery club around £700.

Tuesday 3rd August 1999.

The Scottish manufacturer of a new syringe and needle system which promised to be safer for health workers, received support from a UK cabinet minister as Foreign Secretary and MP for Livingston, Robin Cook, saw the new retractable system when he visited the NMT Group in Livingston. There had been growing concern about the number of so-called needle-stick injuries suffered by health service staff. The Labour politician was on a tour of the factory which was in his own constituency. The redesigned syringes were already on trial at St John's Hospital, and the NMT Group was already working on orders from America.

Wednesday 4th August 1982.
One of the best known double-glazing companies in the country announced that it was opening a new factory facility in Scotland, and that it had chosen Livingston. Everest said that sixty jobs would be created initially, with the workforce hopefully rising to 200 within the next two years. The news was most welcome at the time, as Livingston was becoming a jobs black-spot amid the backdrop of the bleak years of Tory rule.

Tuesday 5th August 1986.
A local group using the acronym LACE called for a council meeting, due to be held that week, to be postponed to give them more time to lodge their objections to plans to build new houses, shops and a primary school along the Murieston Water-Valley- what we would now know simply as 'Murieston'. LACE described the plans as 'social vandalism' and one of their other objections, in addition to environmental concerns, was that the proposed new houses would all be for private sale. They labeled the housing aspect of the plans as 'a private housing ghetto'.

Saturday 6th August 2005.
Livingston's long-serving Labour MP Robin Cook, who had held several top positions within Labour's Government before resigning over the 2003 invasion of Iraq, suffered a heart attack and died whilst out walking with his wife Gaynor near Ben Stack in Sutherland. A post-mortem revealed that the popular politician had been suffering from severe hypertension.

Thursday 7th August 2003.
Over 100 people were arrested in a seven-day crackdown on violent behaviour and drunken youths in West Lothian, Police announced today. They also seized sharpened screwdrivers, deliberately snapped pool cues and knives, in an operation aimed at reducing crime during the summer months. Officers also recovered drugs, including cannabis and amphetamines, and even two stolen cars. The arrests were for a range of offences including offensive

weapons, drug possession with intent to supply, road traffic offences, breaches of the peace and outstanding warrant arrests.

Saturday 8th August 1991.

A scheduled performance by two male-stripper troops called 'The Men of Malibu' and 'The Men of Texas', due to go ahead at Melville's disco, was cancelled after local licensing officers visited the venue to remind them of the local bye-laws regarding nudity or near-nudity in West Lothian places of entertainment. The Council were in-turn blasted as 'boring old fuddy-duddies' by a local group of women calling themselves 'Twenty Bored Ladywell Housewives'. The bye-law had been brought in some ten years earlier, to 'discourage obscenity in the town', as one Councilor said. To this day, that law is the reason why there have been no strip-clubs in Livingston.

Sunday 8th August 2004.

After years of dereliction, the pitch and putt building next to the River Almond was burned to the ground by arsonists. The local council were left with no other option but to demolish it. West Lothian council planned to build a multi million pound civic centre on the site instead.

Sunday 9th August 1981.

A startling discovery was made by a member of the public walking near the viaduct at Oakbank, East Calder. Some person, or persons, had killed one of the farmer's sheep and tried to eat the poor creature. Its mangled corpse was found by teenagers who had been camping nearby. The general consensus at the time was that the poor sheep had been killed by some punks who had also been camping near the viaduct. The woolly 'murder mystery' was never solved.

Friday 9th August 1991.

A gang of audacious thieves stole nearly £200,000 worth of booze from IDV's warehouse in Deans Industrial Estate. CID said that the raid had been meticulously planned, and that at least two vans had been used to 'spirit' the stolen goods away. IDV stated publicly that they would continue trading, and would do everything in their power to ensure that no customers' orders would be affected by the theft. CID appealed for information.

Tuesday 10th August 1999.

An American drugs company announced that it was to double its workforce in Scotland by creating another 1000 jobs, with Livingston set to be the main beneficiary. Quintiles, which already operated three centres in West Lothian, worked for some of the world's largest pharmaceutical companies, developing and testing drugs. The firm at the time was a global enterprise which employed nearly 20,000 people in 31 countries. It supplied a full range of drugs development services, like pre-clinical testing, to some of the world's largest pharmaceutical companies. In Bathgate, 300 people worked as chemists and statisticians providing data management services, while the company chose Livingston to site its UK drugs manufacturing base. A call centre, which recruited and monitored volunteers to test new drugs, was also based in Livingston.

Thursday 11th August 2011.

A Chinese illegal immigrant caught growing cannabis plants worth £30,000 was jailed for two years at Livingston Sheriff Court. He had been in charge of making sure a cannabis farm in Livingston produced the class B drug on a commercial scale, as prices for the herbal version of the drug had recently rocketed, making the trade in the substance almost twice as lucrative. Police had suspected that the house in the Dedridge area was being used as a cannabis farm for some time. The accused was to be deported upon completion of his sentence.

Tuesday 12th August 1337.

The Battle of Blackburn was fought just outside what is now Livingston. Part of the 'War of the Disinherited', it was a rare success for the occupation forces of Edward III and his satellite forces. It was a small heavy-cavalry action which nearly resulted in the capture of Sir William Douglas of Lothian, a relatively minor baron who, through steady military success, had became a noted leader of the Scots in the 1330s and 1340s.

Tuesday 13th August 1991.

A defiant pensioner from Craigshill vowed that she would not budge from, or be intimidated by fire-raisers into leaving, her Jesperson style flat in Craigshill. This was in spite of the fact that her safety was in jeopardy as she continued a long-running dispute with her landlords. The block of flats, of which she was the last remaining tenant, was due to be demolished to make way for a new multi-million pound development. The seventy-two year-old was thought to be at risk after a recent fire in her otherwise abandoned stair. She had lived in the flat, her home, for fifteen years, and vowed only to move if she was given a suitable pensioners' cottage elsewhere in Livingston.

Saturday 14th August 2004.

Leading retail chain Sports World today announced plans to open a 10,000sq ft stand-alone warehouse branch at the Almondvale Retail Park in Livingston. At the time, Sports World was the UK's fastest growing sports retailer, with seven stores in Scotland and 160 in England and Wales. It was hoped that the new venture would create over fifty jobs in the town.

Friday 15th August 2009.

Youths shouting 'USA, USA' threw stones at Craigshill Mosque, causing some minor damage to the building. Two days later, the Mosque was petrol-bombed by a local teenager, who was subsequently caught and fined £400 at court and was also ordered to pay £60 in compensation to the Mosque. The petrol-bomb itself had caused little damage, and its flames were easily stamped out by the Imam. The half-hearted nature of the attack and the fact that the court didn't consider it to be racially motivated were factors in the offender not being given a custodial sentence. There had been opposition to the building of the Mosque in Craigshill ever since its construction had been announced. This can partly be explained, but not excused, by the wave of Islamaphobia which swept Britain following the July 2007 terror attacks in London and the botched attack on Glasgow Airport in the same year.

Friday 16th August 1996.
The Paralympic games in Atlanta, Georgia, USA, began. In these games Livingston's Stephen Payton followed on from his huge success at Berlin's 1994 World Championships, where he had won three gold medals, by winning a bronze medal in the 4 x 100m relay, and smashing a world record to win the gold in the 400m. The super-runner continued his impressive successes right up until the 2008 Paralympics in China, and is deservedly one of Livingston's most famous athletes.

Saturday 17th August 1996.
'Phase two' of Almondvale Shopping Centre opened, hugely improving the town's retail capacity and promising hundreds of new jobs in the town, with its three big stores and 41 smaller retail units.

Saturday 18th August 1979.
An inspirational local schoolgirl took her first fencing lesson at Deans Community High School. The fifteen year-old girl from Ladywell had lost the use of her legs when aged just twelve, after complications following an operation, and used a wheelchair to get around. She joined her able-bodied sister at the fencing club.

Thursday 19th August 1999.
Five children and three adults were being treated in hospital after escaping from a fire in their home in Craigshill. The youngsters and their parents jumped from a first floor window and were caught by a neighbour when the alarm was raised at their house. The children, aged between five and twelve, and their parents were taken to St John's Hospital where they were treated for the effects of smoke inhalation. A neighbour who helped the family jump to safety was being treated for a back injury. It was said that the smoke-alarms in the house had not been connected properly.

Sunday 20th August 2005.

The body of an eleven year-old boy who had been missing for three days was found by a police search team in woods at the west end of Dechmont law, between Deans and the M8 motorway. The boy had died of strangulation and a murder-hunt was soon underway. He had last been seen being dropped off at Meldrum Primary School at 8.30am on the Thursday, and the alarm had been raised seven hours later when a relative arrived to collect him from school only to discover that he hadn't been in class that day. Among the many tributes left where the boy's body was found, was a bouquet of roses with a card attached, bearing the simple but poignant message that summed up the feelings of the town – it just said 'Why?'

Saturday 21st August 1909.

German engineers opened a new Shale-Mine at Dedridge, which, ironically, ended up supplying some of the oil used by British Navy Dreadnoughts during Britain's war with Germany 1914-1918. The mine was closed ten years later in 1919.

Friday 22nd August 1986.

Cash-strapped Livingston United were denied permission to hold an open-air market in a car-park adjacent to their stadium, in a bid to raise funds. District Councilors decided to adhere to LDC'S 'No Markets' policy and also took into consideration a number of complaints from locals and from the police. The club was, however, granted permission, as a concession, to hold fortnightly car-boot sales for a three month trial period, in an attempt to help the struggling club get back on its feet. At the time, Livingston United were on the brink of going bust, but it was thought that they could easily save themselves by simply getting another fifty or so paying customers to attend their home games.

Friday 23rd August 1991.

LDC became one of the first councils in the country to introduce tough new measures aimed at fighting racial discrimination. LDC said that 'racial harassment would not be tolerated and swift action will be taken whenever such incidents occur.' However, their plans to keep a special record of serious racist incidents were condemned by three LDC board members, one of whom claimed that there was 'no evidence that the victims of these crimes would want such a record to be kept'. LDC's leadership hit back at the three dissenters, pointing out that keeping such records was a requirement forced upon the LDC by central government.

Wednesday 24th August 1988.

Livingston's two SNP Councilors accused LDC of 'operating a two-tier housing system' that encouraged the creation of 'Toffs only' housing developments. They accused LDC of spending £500,000 of public money on buying twenty houses in the Easter-Bankton/Murieston areas. One of the SNP men said that the public were excluded from applying for these houses, which he said had been reserved for short-term use for highly-paid incoming workers, either as short-term lets or with a view to buying. LDC played down the claims, claiming that the amount of money involved was insignificant, but the SNP men hit back, by pointing out that £500,000 was certainly not an insignificant amount to the average Livingstonian, many of whom were stuck on the council's long housing waiting list and were desperate for new homes.

Saturday 25th August 1979.

A talented young footballer from Deans, aged just eighteen, who had once been given a trial with Rangers, collapsed and died of a heart attack shortly after being substituted twenty minutes into his debut for Craigshill Eagles against Whitburn Bluebell. He was given the kiss of life at the scene and attended by paramedics, but to no avail, and he sadly never regained consciousness.

Friday 26th August 1963.

In Livingston Village, The Secretary of State for Scotland symbolically pulled the lever of a pile-driver, thus commencing construction of the new LDC office block. Almost the entire population of the village was in attendance, along with around 150 invited guests and dignitaries. Mr. Noble, the Secretary of State, also announced plans to build 250 new houses for workers employed by the BMC factory at nearby Bathgate.

Thursday 26th August 1979.

A supposed would-be burglar's body was discovered upside down in a ventilator shaft at The Centre, after shoppers complained about a putrid smell. It was believed that the body had been wedged there for about three weeks. The body was bloated and blue and its head had swollen to almost twice its normal size. A rather insensitive Livingston policeman described the man as looking like 'Idi Amin with his face smashed in'.

Tuesday 27th August 1991.

Livingston's tax-payers were told they faced a £13,000 repair bill after two teenagers smashed 175 windows at Harrysmuir Primary School in Ladywell. However, on this day, one of the teenagers walked free from court after paying just £180 compensation to the school, and a baffled sheriff said that he 'could not understand why such a small sum' apiece had been imposed on the pair when they had first appeared in court the previous November, when they had admitted to smashing the windows with hammers. The other teen walked free after having paid just £50, the reason being that his temporary job had ended the previous Christmas, though he was ordered to appear before the court in one month's time, after social background reports had been compiled.

Friday 28th August 1987.

LDC received a grant of £50,000 from central government to put towards cultural projects in the town, to be spread out over the following three years. Among the groups who benefited were:

Livingston Brass Band - £3000 per year.
Livingston and Pumpherston Pipe Band - £1500 per year.
Livingston and District Athletic Club -£1000 per year.
Dedridge Dolphins Swimming Club - £100 per year.
Tocata Ladies' Choir - £700 per year.
Livingston Rugby Club - £1000 per year.

Livingston United FC - £1500 in year one, then £300 a year for the next two years.

Thursday 29th August 2002.
A tedious encounter at Almondvale saw Livingston draw 0-0 with FC Vaduz of Liechtenstein in the UEFA Cup. The Lions went through to the next round thanks to the away-goals rule, having drawn 1-1 in the away leg.

Monday 30th August 1982.
Sick, mindless morons went on a vandalism spree – in the cemetery at Livingston Village. Headstones were kicked over and snapped in the Kirk-Lane graveyard, and the violence was swiftly condemned by local residents and the local councilor, Terry Coleman. Police undertook extensive door-to-door enquiries in an attempt to catch the sickos. Council workers were brought in that very morning to begin repairing the damage. Witnesses later said that they had seen children playing football in the cemetery a few days before the vandalism occurred.

Saturday 30th August 1986.
Three senior pupils from Inveralmond High School, who had made a short film about the war on drugs, were given an award for their film 'A mug's game'. At an award ceremony on this day, they were won the Grundig Award for best school film, and also came second in the overall national competition, run by The Federation of British Tape Recorders.

Thursday 31st August 1967.
A survey of 1000 employees by LDC to establish more about the town's changing demographic of workers, revealed the following results.
Managers/Executives of large businesses – 40
Managers/Owners of small businesses with less than 25 employees – 7
Self-employed – 101
Intermediate Non manual workers – 64

Junior Non Manual Workers – 91
Personal Service Workers – 6
Foremen/Industrial Supervisors – 48
Skilled Manual Workers - 381
Semi-Skilled Manual Workers - 146
Unskilled Manual Workers – 63
Own Account Workers – 2
Farmers - 2
Agricultural Workers – 13
Other/Unable to classify – 36

SEPTEMBER

Friday 1st September 1979.
A fifty-one year-old man managed to bluff his way out of being mugged at knifepoint whilst crossing the footbridge between Dedridge and Mid Calder. Two men simply described as 'Yobs' approached the man with a pen-knife and demanded money. The man coolly informed the yobs that he had a much bigger blade in his back pocket, and asked them if they wanted to see it, whereupon the terrified yobs ran off. The man, who hadn't really been carrying a knife, went home and phoned the police. He later said that 'No way were they getting a penny out of me'.

Wednesday 2nd September 1668.
Sir Patrick Murray, renowned early botanist and the owner of the Peel Tower, left the Livingston area to see the world and further his botany studies in France and Holland. On his travels he gained many new ideas regarding the use of canals that he hoped to bring back to Scotland, but alas, he caught a ghastly fever at Avignon whilst on his way to Italy in 1671, and died, aged just 39.

Sunday 3rd September 2000.
A 32-year-old woman from Knightsridge died of her injuries in hospital after a car accident in Livingston. She suffered head injuries after the car in which she was a passenger hit a lamp-post early on the Saturday morning near the Lizzie Bryce Roundabout. A report was sent to the Procurator Fiscal.

Friday 4th September 2009.
It was announced today that 500 jobs would be lost in Livingston, as Bausch & Lomb said it planned to shut its facility at Kirkton Campus and shift production to Ireland and the United States. The firm said it planned to shift its hi-tech contact lens production to Waterford in Ireland and to Rochester in New York. It

expected to have fully withdrawn from Livingston by 2011. The Scottish government pledged to fight the move vigorously.

Thursday 5th September 1991.

A twenty-three year-old Postman from Dedridge appeared in court, charged with stealing mail from his own round. The Fiscal told how five discarded letters had been found on the postman's route on a path between Bellsquarry and Dedridge, so a test package containing a birthday card and a wad of cash had been planted on the man's round, and had subsequently failed to arrive at its destination. When confronted by his bosses, the postman had owned up, and a search of his home later uncovered several more stolen letters. He pleaded guilty in court, and was given a community service sentence.

Friday 6th September 1996.

A new out of town Retail Village was opened between West Calder and Blackburn, against the backdrop of the Five Sisters Bings. Named 'Freeport', it mostly consisted of factory outlets for various designer clothing brands. The site did reasonably well at first, but was hampered by poor travel links, and by the opening of Phase Two of Livingston Centre. By March 2001 only six of its sixty units still traded, and the shops there closed soon afterwards amid plummeting footfall. Since it ceased operations as a retail unit, the site and its empty buildings have been used for many things, including car-boot sales, paintball, Airsoft, Police firearms training and anti-terrorism exercises by the Scottish Ambulance Service/SORT.

Sunday 6th September 1998.

A woman of 59 in a Volkswagen Polo was killed in a car crash in Deans East, near Westwood Park, Deans. Her husband, who was driving the car, suffered serious chest injuries. Police appealed for witnesses.

Wednesday 7th September 2011.

A forty-eight year-old man appeared at Livingston Sheriff Court accused of trying to blow up his former girlfriend's house by turning on the gas supply and setting fire to the furniture. The man, a spurned lover, was said to have put the lives of fire and ambulance crews at risk as well as the safety of his ex. He had pressed a cushion over her mouth and brandished a knife at her before setting fire to her home during the terrifying incident on March 7th. Then later, when sent for psychiatric evaluation at St John's, he threatened to kill one of the nurses. He was given fourteen-months in prison.

Thursday 8th September 1334.
Sir Richard Talbot and a company of English knights and men-at-arms were attacked by a Scottish force under Sir William Keith, in what we would now call the Bathgate Hills. The English were eventually compelled to surrender at a church near Linlithgow. Talbot had to raise an enormous ransom of £2000 to secure his liberty.

Sunday 8th September 1991.
A major-fundraising event was held at Letham Bowling Club in Craigshill, as part of a wider campaign across Lothian to raise funds for The Sick Kids' Hospital in Edinburgh. This particular event however, had significance locally, as one of the club's junior members was a thirteen year-old girl from Howden who attended Craigshill High School, who was fighting a courageous battle against Leukaemia at the time and was actually being treated at the hospital. The Bowling Club's open day consisted of a sponsored bowling competition, and various stalls and raffles, from which it was hoped to help buy the hospital two expensive but vital infusion pumps, costing £1500 each.

Wednesday 9th September 1998.
Houston Industrial Estate in Livingston was sold by Highcross, a private investment and development company, to clients of PRICOA Property Investment Management Ltd. The price of £7m reflected the estate's value. The estate was acquired by Highcross in 1994 during the wind up of Livingston Development Corporation. Close to Junction 3 of the M8, at the time it consisted of 38 industrial and warehouse units. Current rental income then stood at around

£780,000 per annum. On the same day, a single unit at Kirkton Campus was also sold, fetching £500,000.

Friday 10th September 1920.
A much-loved school-teacher at Livingston Station School, Miss Muir, was killed in a tragic motor-car accident whilst on her way home from work.

Tuesday 11th September 1979.
A thirty year-old man, who had just got himself a temporary job working on a Waltzer ride in Livingston, was hurled into the air and then caught under and dragged around the fifty-foot diameter Waltzer turntable four times before it could be stopped. The man, originally from Harthill, was rushed to Bangour Hospital with a broken leg, fractured ribs and concussion, in what was a miraculous escape.

Saturday 11th September 1999.
A match at Livingston's Station Park received two unwanted supporters. The football game was between local side Broxburn Colts, who played in maroon, and Edinburgh side Edina Hibs. The two unwanted supporters were drunken men in their early twenties who stood on one of the tiny terraces roaring Hibs songs whilst drinking Buckfast, to the mirth of some spectators and players, but much to the annoyance of everyone else. Edina Hibs were nothing to do with Hibernian at that time, even though they wore the SPL side's colours. The aggressive, drunken singing continued until the two young men saw a police car approaching the stadium, whereupon they swiftly departed.

Friday 12th September 1941.
A seriously botched raid on Edinburgh by The Luftwaffe saw a lone German bomber chased by the RAF into the skies above Livingston, where it dropped two of its bombs, hurting no-one but causing two enormous craters near Livingston Station. The bomber escaped. The irony of this incident was that twenty-four child evacuees from Edinburgh and Glasgow were living in Livingston

Station at the time, where they had been sent to escape the expected bombing carnage that Hitler had threatened would flatten Britain's cities.

Thursday 12th September 1991.

Livingston Police were asked to compile a special report by West Lothian Council, as part of a nationwide campaign to stamp out 'undesirable' elements from Scotland's streets. The main targets of the report were said to be 'Drunks, football casuals and teenage tearaways.' It was hoped that the findings of the report would give police and councils new powers with which to clean up the streets. The main cause of the 'problem' was said to be the repeal sixteen years earlier of the 1892 Burgh's Police Scotland Act. When published, the report recommended that drinking in the street, playing football in the street, and hanging around in groups in the street, be made illegal. A representative of a Knightsridge community group said 'People are sick of street-louts drinking, street football, and Gala-days that are supposed to be for kids being hijacked by swearing, drunken morons', but he added 'we don't want some sort of Draconian approach to these problems, we just want Bobbies on the beat to be given more powers to deal with these pressing issues.'

Sunday 13th September 1987.

David Murray's MIM Livingston Basketball team narrowly defeated Oldham Celtics at The Forum, in what was their first match in the new British Basketball League, having already trounced all Scottish opponents that they encountered in domestic competitions. Basketball never really took off in Livingston - for many, it was one step towards Americanisation too far.

Tuesday 14th September 1745.

Some of Prince Charles Edward Stuart's officers spent the night in a country manor which is now buried underneath Pumpherston Bing, during the Jacobites' advance on Edinburgh, after earlier routing English Dragoons at Coatbridge . The word 'Bing' is simply an Anglicised version of the Gaelic word for hill – Beinn or Ben.

While in West Lothian, the Jacobites managed to raise a small troop of cavalry which they called 'Kilmarnock's Horse Guards', after the regiment's colonel, Lord Kilmarnock. They fought at Culloden on foot, as by then they had been forced to turn over their horses to the more experienced Franco-Irish cavalrymen of Fitz-James' Horse, a regular unit.

Thursday 15th September 1987.
Armed robbers stole over £75,000 from Bank of Scotland's Carmondean branch. Two men stormed into the building at 5.27pm – three minutes before closing time- armed with a shotgun and a claw-hammer. One of then jumped the security screen and started taking cash, while the other man held the terrified staff and customers at gunpoint. A third man was waiting outside in a getaway car, which the three robbers then escaped in. The car was later found, burned out, at the back of MacMillans' Bar in Deans. (Rab's bar)

Saturday 16th September 2000.
Amid a series of national strikes and protests over fuel prices, mostly instigated by lorry drivers and farmers, the people of Livingston, and the staff at Forth FM, were the victims of an imaginative but hilarious hoax. With most petrol stations in Lothian out of fuel, someone claiming to be from Almond West Service Station, next to the dual-carriageway, rang up Forth FM to tell them that they had 'full stocks of petrol and diesel' and even mentioned a special 'fill your tank for fifty quid' offer. Forth FM, in all innocence, relayed this news to the masses, and within an hour, dozens of cars were driving towards the aforementioned garage in Craigshill – which in reality had had its petrol pumps removed and had stopped selling fuel more than five years previously. Cars circled the old garage – which was by then just a convenience store, for several hours before Forth FM were notified about the windup and told their listeners about it.

Tuesday 17th September 2002.
Plans to trial '20mph villages' in West Lothian looked set to be given the go-ahead. The new advisory speed limit restrictions were

about to be tested in Boghall, Mid Calder and Polbeth as well as parts of East Calder, Howden, Ladywell and Broxburn.

West Lothian Council was to pay for the £150,000 project with funding from the Scottish Executive. By introducing the pilot scheme, the council was responding to concerns raised by West Lothian residents about speeding, particularly in areas where children played.

Friday 18th September 2009.

An emergency exercise taking place today helped ensure that Scotland was ready to face the risks resulting from a major terrorist incident. It involved around 700 people drawn from the police, fire and ambulance services, including 250 volunteer members of the public, and eight amputee stunt-men. Exercise Green Gate enabled the emergency services to train together and practice with the specialist decontamination equipment that they would use in the event of the release of hazardous materials, such as an explosion by a 'dirty' bomb. The exercise was held in the grounds of the old Bangour Hospital.

Saturday 19th September 1987.

Some eighty youths from Livingston took a short bus journey to Bathgate, where they promptly started a full-scale riot in the town centre, a rampage that lasted until midnight. Terrified pedestrians were said to have been knocked to the ground, and two policemen were assaulted as Bathgate's youths battled it out with Livingston's. There were numerous arrests and eight of those accused of being responsible for the carnage were later remanded in custody after appearing in court.

Saturday 20th September 1986.

A battle of the bands was one of the first big musical events at Livingston Forum, judged by LDC officials. The venue had opened only a few weeks previously and was owned by LDC, but was first operated by a leisure company owned by Rangers chairman David Murray, who also attended the building's official opening. The huge multi-purpose venue (it was an unofficial civic centre as well as an events venue) resembled a huge World War Two Anderson Bomb Shelter from the outside. For years it was to serve the town well and is probably best remembered for the 'Awesome 101' and 'Dance-Mania' rave events held there in the 90's. It was demolished in 1999.

Wednesday 20th September 1995.

Livingston FC won their first ever home league match since being rebranded from the old Meadowbank Thistle, beating Queens Park 2-0 at Almondvale in Bells Division Three. The Lions eventually won the title that season, losing only six league matches.

Friday 21st September 1991.

Craigshill High School's enraged students found out that their school was to close in the latest round of Tory cuts, and that they themselves were to be transferred to Inveralmond High School in Ladywell. That afternoon, about one-hundred Craigshill High students staged a lock in and riot. Some students barricaded themselves into the school's social area, while others went outside and, using bricks ripped from the slope outside the school P.E block, set off hundreds of 'Hilti' mini-explosive caps that they had liberated from a local building site. Amid the banging of the Hiltis and the temporary takeover of the social area, teaching staff were, for a time, utterly impotent and unable to restore order, resorting to standing with notepads taking down names of those involved in the protest, and they were simply ignored by the students. At the time, quasi-gang warfare that periodically existed between Craigshill and every other adjoining district of Livingston was rife, and many Craigshill High students were understandably concerned about merging schools with who they saw at the time as their bitter rivals. A popular spokesman for the students called Frank told the West Lothian Courier that 'We'll be coming back from Inveralmond in body bags', and that summed up exactly how most Craigshill High students felt. In the end, the transition to merging schools was largely uneventful, partly because Inveralmond's students were sternly warned against antagonising the 'new arrivals', but also because when put in the same school together, most students realised that they weren't really that different from one another. Ultimately, over time, this school merger eradicated much of the inter-district rivalry and fighting and was in some ways a masterstroke, socially, though most Craigshill High pupils always lamented the loss of their beloved school. The Craigshill High site was soon sold to housing developers, with the exception of the P.E block which has since been converted to use as a community gymnastics centre.

Wednesday 21st September 2005.
High-flying Hearts, top of the league and thus far unbeaten, suffered a humiliation as they were bundled out of the League Cup by Livingston at Almondvale, the only goal of the game being scored by former Hearts player Ramon Pereira.

Thursday 22nd September 1988.
A Livingston man appeared in the local paper and described allegations that he planned to open a 'glorified doss-house' at Newyearfield as 'appalling'. The developer, who lived in Livingston Village, planned to spend over £300,000 on a small hotel at the site between what is now Ladywell-West and Eliburn. His hotel was actually intended to provide short-term accommodation for sales reps, businessmen and lorry drivers who needed a place to stay in the town. The hotel would be modest but would have double-glazing, central heating and would be well insulated. The 'doss-house' allegation had been made by a local councilor, who objected to the development on the grounds that the lands might be better used for something else. A development eventually went ahead on the site, and you will probably recognise it simply as, Da Vinci's.

Thursday 23rd September 1982.
Around fifty angry, unemployed young people marched through Livingston, protesting about the large scale of youth unemployment in the country and at the lack of jobs available locally. The march formed part of a trek from Edinburgh to Glasgow, with a one-night stopover in Bathgate. Carrying placards, the group arrived at The Mall in Craigshill before marching to Deans. On their way they paid a visit to Cameron Iron Works, where they had a meeting with shop-stewards. The march had been organised by the STUC and NUS. It

was flanked by police all the way through Livingston, and later, Police said that the marchers had all behaved themselves.

Wednesday 24th September 1986.

Livingston's famous 'Woolco' store closed its doors for the last time, much to the lamentation of townsfolk and LDC alike. This meant that Livingston's Christmas shoppers would have no large store to shop at in the town over the festive season.

Wednesday 25th September 1963.

Cameron Iron-Works announced that they were opening a huge forge and workshop in Houston Industrial Estate. When first conceived, it was planned that it would employ over 2000 workers. Clearly visible from the dual-carriageway, it is one of Livingston's truly iconic buildings.

Tuesday 25th September 1979.

LDC learned, with considerable relief, that it was not to face the axe in the new Tory government's latest round of savage, ideologically driven spending cuts. The Secretary of State for Scotland said that he had 'no intention of doing away with any of the new towns' councils'. The main advocate of doing away with the new towns all over Britain was Tory Minister Michael Heseltine. In retrospect, this was one of the most important decisions in Livingston's history.

Thursday 26th September 2002.

Sickos broke into a children's nursery and tortured and killed its pet Guinea Pig - then left its body strung up on a barbed wire fence. The horrific incident happened at the Jack and Jill nursery in Livingston. It was said that the pre-school youngsters were 'devastated' by the loss of a second much-loved pet, who they called Cinnamon. It was the second time in a few months that the nursery had been targeted. In May of the same year, the same sickos broke in and played football with the nursery's first Guinea Pig, Salt n Pepper, before cruelly stamping it to death.

Monday 27th September 1982.

At a packed public meeting in the Toronto Community Wing in Howden, residents unanimously backed a motion protesting against a proposed pub in Howden's Kingsport Avenue. The residents feared that a pub would attract undesirable elements to Howden, and one resident said that he feared the locale would become a battlefield at closing time. The proposed pub would have been built on the site of the old DHSS building beside St Andrew's Primary School. The school itself was also firmly against the move. The pub was never built, and Howden has remained the only district of Livingston not to contain a public house. Some Livingstonians argue that Howden has always been a little bit quieter and a little bit tidier, precisely because of its 'dry' status.

Wednesday 28th September 1985.

A factory in Houston Industrial Estate was targeted by vandals-come-copper thieves. The huge factory, which made materials for the building trade, was broken into by a gang of youths, thought to be from one of the nearby districts of Livingston. Much copper was stripped from its fittings, then the youths started destroying the factory, smashing lights, breaking things and tearing down signs. Then, when the vandals started to smash up the factory's fuse-box, it short circuited and began to belch smoke. The vandals had to hurriedly vacate the premises without any stolen metal, and narrowly missed being killed as the short-circuit caused part of the factory to explode. The destruction had another consequence – the short-circuit and small explosion overloaded a nearby electricity sub-station, meaning that Pumpherston and Uphall Station suffered a power-cut for a number of hours. The factory wasn't completely destroyed by the explosion, and no-one was hurt. The company in question left Livingston soon afterwards. The vandals, thought to be from Knightsridge or Pumpherston, were never caught.

Thursday 29th September 1988.

After a very close-run vote at LDC, permission was finally granted to the couple from Livingston Village who wanted to build a hotel at Newyearfield. In the years since, the area has become something of a mini-village, with hotel, cheesy bar, shops and restaurants, as well as new housing. But if it hadn't been for these developers, and some more forward-thinking members of LDC, who knows what might stand on the site today.

Friday 30th September 1977.

'Woolco', one of the most remembered shops from the town's past, opened its doors for the first time, in Livingston Centre. It proved an instant hit with Livingstonians.

OCTOBER

Friday 1st October 2004.
Deans South residents, including 85 who owned their homes, received a letter from West Lothian Council advising them that the houses were unsafe and that they would have to be demolished. Many of the homes had unsafe fire insulation, leaking roofs, unstable walls and rotting timbers. All Council residents were to have been moved to new housing, but some of the housing remained occupied after the council's derisory offers to buy their homes were rejected by 69 of the 85 homeowners.

Friday 2nd October 1987.
Livingston pub The Paraffin Lamp made it into the top 100 best designed taverns list for Scotland. The award was sponsored by Guinness. The pub was praised for its 'innovative interior design' by the judging panel of minor celebrities and industry experts. No, this isn't a joke.

Wednesday 3rd October 1979.
A drunken man from Livingston threw a brick through the windows of The Masonic Arms in Broxburn – in full view of a police officer. The man intended no malice towards the establishment, he later said, but rather, was so drunk that he couldn't be bothered walking home to his house in Livingston. He got his 'wish'; he was arrested and spent the night in a dank cell in Broxburn Police Station.

Thursday 3rd October 2002.
Valiant Livingston defeated Austrian side Sturm Graz 4-3 in a thrilling match at Almondvale in the UEFA Cup. Sadly, The Lions were eliminated from the tournament 8-6 on aggregate after their 2-5 hammering in the first leg at the Arnold Schwarzenegger Stadium.

Monday 4th October 2004.

A mob of youths attacked a fire crew who were called to put out a wheelie bin blaze in Knightsridge. Having brought the fire under control, the crew was just starting to clear up the mess left by the melted bin when they were attacked by a gang hurling stones at them. As the firefighters turned round to see where the missiles had come from, they saw children pedaling off on bikes. A spokesman for Lothian and Borders Fire Brigade said there had already been 28 cases of fire crews being attacked since January.

Saturday 5th October 1996.

DF Concerts brought Welsh rockers The Manic Street Preachers to Livingston Forum. Tickets were £10 to see the popular political rockers. The Forum was later demolished in 1999, leaving Livingston without a 'proper' concert venue ever since.

Saturday 6th October 1984.

Livingston South Train Station, at Murieston and on the main Glasgow-Edinburgh line, was opened by the area's local councilor. It was hoped that this new travel link would be of great use to the people of Livingston, both for work and for leisure trips.

Wednesday 7th October 1998.

The American company Seagate Microelectronics announced that its factory in Livingston was up for sale, with the potential loss of up to 275 jobs. Workers were called to a mass meeting at the plant by senior managers, where they were given the bad news. The plant employed some 275 workers who made the same type of silicon chip 'wafers' manufactured by the troubled company National Semiconductors.

Friday 8th October 1982.

Single parent families in Livingston received a welcome boost with the opening of a new support centre, run by the voluntary organisation, Gingerbread. The centre, in Craigshill's Adelaide Street, was intended to help one-parent families come to terms with their problems. The three-apartment building was initially staffed by two workers who were actually on an MSC scheme. The centre was funded by LDC.

Thursday 9th October 1986.

The recently installed Minister for New Towns, Ian Lang, met with representatives of SLANT (Scottish Local Authorities with New Towns), who pleaded with the minister that Livingston needed at least 200 houses to be built every year to cope with the pressures on the current waiting list. They warned Mr. Lang that if these pleas were ignored, Livingston would have a shortfall of 1800 houses within the next two years.

Wednesday 10th October 1979.

It was announced that Craigshill High School was to be used as a youth-facility for four evenings of every week. It was hoped that provision of this 'Youth Club' would give the town's HUGE under 20's population something constructive to do in the evenings. Hitherto, there had been little for the town's youngsters to do, except play football or hang around the streets outwith school hours, and this had resulted in an upward trend across the town for graffiti, micro-gang warfare between districts, vandalism, glue-sniffing and general anti-social behaviour.

Tuesday 11th October 1988.

Although there wasn't a hamburger in site, fast-food chain Wimpy opened their new warehouse facility at Deans Industrial Estate. Nine staff were employed at the new site at first, the warehouse being needed by Wimpy amid the rise of the fast-food industry, which had seen Wimpy's turnover in Scotland alone increase by 100%. The new warehouse was three times the size of Wimpy's old Livingston depot. Over the years, Wimpy was eclipsed by Burger King and McDonalds, and later had to rely on outside distributers like 3663 at Newbridge and Holroyd Meek to supply its outlets, as its growth turned into a rapid decline that would see it virtually disappear.

Tuesday 12th October 1982.

Livingston's CND spokesman, Martin Togneri, claimed in an interview that nearly three-quarters of Livingston's population would be killed instantly if a nuclear bomb or missile hit the town. The rather obvious statement was part of a campaign against the government's 'Hardrock' campaign, its plan to deal with a possible Soviet nuclear attack. Hardrock itself was abandoned shortly afterwards for other reasons. CND's main concerns had been the lack of provision of a nuclear shelter for ordinary civilians (the bunker at East Calder was for government officials and staff, the rich, aristocrats and the select few people that the government deemed essential in the event of an attack, it wasn't for the public) and the proposed aspect of Hardrock that called for judiciary powers to be given directly to the police and the army in the event of an attack. The latter caused great concern to CND in Livingston, as they speculated that, with no courts or prisons available after a nuclear attack, people would be put to death for any infraction, because there was no alternative if order was to be preserved.

Saturday 13th October 1906.

Bangour Hospital was opened by the Earl of Rosebury, Lord Lieutenant of Linlithgowshire, amid much pomp and ceremony. In its time it has been both a general hospital and a mental hospital, but is best known for its pioneering treatment of burns victims during the World Wars. It closed in 1991, and its deserted buildings are believed to contain dangerously high levels of asbestos. The site is periodically used by The Scottish Government and Scottish Ambulance Service for training exercises. It is also believed to be haunted.

Friday 13th October 1989.

Craigshill Social Club was the setting for one of the most famous incidents in Livingston's history. A loan-shark who had been making many peoples' lives in Craigshill a misery, even confiscating benefit books and prams from single mothers, was taken into a room in the Social Club by who most people in Livingston consider to be a local hero, or heroes, and shot in the legs whilst begging for mercy.

Despite the club being filled with hundreds of locals, no-one saw or heard anything, and the police, who had let the loan shark terrorise the community with relative impunity, had no witnesses. The good people of Craigshill never suffered at the hands of a loan-shark again. To paraphrase an annoying modern TV advert, 'BANG- and the debt was gone!'

Thursday 14th October 2010.

More than twenty firefighters today continued to fight a fierce blaze which broke out the day before at the Amcor Flexibles printing factory, in Brucefield Industrial Estate near Livingston, creating a plume of smoke visible for miles around and closing a nearby rail line. At its peak, 70 firefighters were battling to control the fire as they faced the added hazard of a potentially lethal cocktail of toxic and volatile chemicals. Three firefighters were taken to St John's Hospital complaining of nausea after breathing in toxic smoke. A further twelve firefighters had to be decontaminated after being exposed to chromic acid, which can cause cancer, skin lesions and ulcers. Another man, who was taken to hospital with burns to his arms, was thought to be an employee who tried to extinguish the blaze, which had started at around midday after three small explosions.

Thursday 15th October 1987.

Raggaty Ann, a three year-old sheep and one of the first animals to be born at Mill Farm, was killed by local sickos, apparently for her meat. Her carcass was discovered by the Park Warden who lamented this, the first instance of vandalism ever suffered by Mill Farm. The Warden also warned that the meat was not fit for human consumption. The Police treated the matter as a theft and said that the sickos involved would have had no problem in enticing the sheep towards their clutches as it was so used to humans. The Sheep had just gotten over a serious illness before this sad episode.

Thursday 16th October 2008.

The new phase of Almondvale Centre, known as 'The Elements' during its construction, had its official opening. It was constructed as six separate buildings brought together with one massive transparent roof, to supposedly create a 'unique' shopping experience. The new extension originally had 35 new shops, restaurants and bars and cost around £150m to construct. Ironically, the shopping centre as a whole is now officially called 'The Centre', which is what the facility was widely referred to as by Livingstonians for decades beforehand anyway.

Thursday 17th October 1977.
A female was found drunk and asleep in bed in Elm Grove in Craigshill. Unluckily for her, it was a flower-bed, and it wasn't her own garden. Police soon arrived at the scene and arrested her, but when they got her to the police station she became aggressive and verbally abusive and was eventually charged with Breach of the Peace, later being fined £5.

Monday 18th October 1915.
The headmaster of Livingston Station School, in what is now Deans, noted in his diary that over 20% of his school's pupils were absent because they were busy helping with the local potato harvest. This level of absence continued for one week, until the harvest was completed.

Friday 19th October 2001.
A Livingston family had their car hi-jacked when they stopped for fuel in Berkshire, England. As mum, dad and older brother popped into the garage, the eight year-old girl remained in the car, the parents having left the car keys in the ignition. The car thief didn't notice that the little-girl was still in the car until he reached nearby Slough, where he quickly dropped her off somewhere that she would be found quickly. The girl was distressed by the incident, but was not physically harmed in any way. Later she said 'he was really a nice man and he just wanted the car'.

Thursday 20th October 1988.

Concerned Ladywell residents learned today that they had failed in their bid to stop Dean Entertainments from being granted a license to open a new pub in the old British Legion building opposite Eagle Brae. Local residents feared a wave of drunkenness, urinating in the street and late-night disturbances, but the pub, which most of us now remember as 'Oscars', got the go-ahead, as there wasn't another bar for over half a mile. It has since been Oscars, then a Chinese Restaurant, but is now a pub again.

Thursday 21st October 1760.

Livingston's oldest pub, The Livingston Inn, located in what is now Livingston Village, was opened for use as an Inn and Coach-House for those traveling from Edinburgh to Glasgow and Kilmarnock.

Monday 22nd October 2007.

Police began searching for a limousine driver who killed a seven-year-old boy in a hit-and- run accident days earlier. The schoolboy died after he was knocked down by the car as he played in the street near his Craigshill home. Witnesses had reported seeing the car swerve before it hit the boy, who is thought to have run into its path. He was taken to the Royal Hospital for Sick Children in Edinburgh where he sadly died shortly after arrival. Police said they had recovered the vehicle, but appealed for help to trace its driver. The site of the incident was soon carpeted with tributes, including flowers, and Celtic and Rangers jerseys.

Friday 23rd October 1987.

A lorry on the M8 motorway crashed into two of the support columns of the dual-carriageway/A899 that carried the carriageway over the busy motorway. The driver wasn't seriously injured. Motorists were told to expect months of intermittent delays in the area as a result of the accident. Emergency metal supports were fitted to the 'bridge' and the northbound carriageway of the dual carriageway was closed for a time, with a contra-flow in operation on the southbound one. The M8 was also closed eastbound for a while as repairs were made.

Friday 24th October 1986.

Three men from Livingston and their accomplice from Edinburgh appeared at Linlithgow Sheriff Court for sentencing and were fined a total of £6500 for an elaborate plot to smuggle 700lbs of tobacco into Scotland from Belgium. They had earlier pleaded guilty to the offence, which if it had been successful, would have deprived the exchequer of nearly £14,000 in tax.

Monday 24th October 1988.

Angry residents of Craigswood, including many pensioners, received the news that they could expect another winter of trying to push trolleys and carry bags up the steep hill to their small housing estate from Brisbane Street bus-stop. This was despite assurances the previous May that Craigswood would get its own bus-stop soon. Craigshill's Councilor Anderson was furious, and issued a tongue-in-cheek invitation to the Lothian Transport Minister to help him to assist pensioners in carrying their messages up the steep hill, to see what it was like for himself. The fury of councilor and residents alike was worsened by the fact that all summer, workmen had been re-aligning kerbs in Craigshill, and had even resurfaced the very road that the bus-stop would, eventually, be located on. The campaign to get a bus stop for Craigswood took eight years.

Monday 25th October 2004.

New procedures to assess how dangerous 'remote' footpaths were in West Lothian were introduced amid growing concern over their safety. Council chiefs were inundated with requests from the public for footpaths to be closed because of the level of vandalism and anti-social behaviour that they attracted. However, in a bid to prevent 'knee jerk' reactions and the closure of busy footpaths, the council today decided to implement a procedure to make sure that all requests for footpath closures were dealt with fairly and consistently. Many paths in the area had become infamous and undercover cops had launched patrols in isolated areas in Livingston to prevent attacks on women. The move came amid fears a gang of violent thugs was targeting clubbers leaving nightspots, to attack and rob them. More than 25 assaults and robberies were reported to police in specific areas of Livingston, including Almondvale, Howden, Ladywell and Craigshill, in one month alone.

Saturday 26th October 1979.
A Livingston couple got more than what they had ordered when they sat down to eat a curry together at a restaurant in Bellsquarry. Their food was found to contain a whole, intact Australian Spider-Beetle, causing great revulsion among the diners. A subsequent enquiry by Environmental Health fined the establishment £10 for the incident.

Sunday 27th October 1979.
Craigshill High School was badly damaged by an arson attack. The school's headmaster, Mr. Pirie, said that the blaze 'could have had awful consequences for the school, because evidence suggested that the fire was started by persons with intricate knowledge of the building's layout', which led him and the police to the conclusion that the fire was started by pupils or ex-pupils of the school. The headmaster described the arsonists' actions as 'wicked and callous'. Two fortunate twists of fate stopped the blaze from destroying the entire school – Firstly, a keen-eyed local spotted the blaze early and dialed 999, secondly, the seat of the fire was below a plastic water pipe, which melted and partially doused the flames with water, buying time for the fire engines from three local stations who attended, and got the blaze under control within just over an hour. No-one was injured in the fire, and an investigation was launched by CID.

Thursday 28th October 1982.
In a nice gesture, The Livingston Post published a picture of a Craigshill man and his family. The man, a Mr. Rintoul, was at the time a radio-operator on board HMS Illustrious, serving his country in the South Atlantic near the Falkland Islands, which had recently been recaptured from Argentina. His fellow radio operator on the

ship was from Dedridge, and the two men had had copies of 'The Post' sent to them throughout their time at sea. Both men were said to have been sick of only being able to get British tabloids while on active service, so their families were sending them the local paper. This edition in particular, must have brought a smile to both men's faces, especially Mr. Rintoul.

Friday 29th October 1756.

The stone bridge over the Almond, at near what is now the bottom of Howden was opened, for the purpose of carrying what was then a toll-road between Kilmarnock/Glasgow and Edinburgh. In those days, it took just over twelve hours to travel from one city to the other.

Sunday 30th October 1988.

Bending and stretching were the order of the day at The Forum, as dozens of people turned up to participate in an aerobics marathon, organised by a local woman in aid of a fourteen year-old burns victim from Edinburgh. The little girl herself was unable to leave her bed at Bangour Burns Unit to attend the event, she had been in that bed for four months, but she was able to watch the event later as it was recorded on video camera. The aerobics certainly sorted the men from the boys, so to speak. Livingston's American Football team, The Chieftains, came along hoping to show everyone else how it was done, but so exhausted themselves in the first session that they were unable to attend the second one. One man who did attend and completed all of the aerobics sessions was Ross Davidson, better known at the time as 'Andy' the Scotsman in Eastenders. He later visited the brave little girl in hospital. His real name was actually William Russell Davidson and he died in 2006 after a long illness. £1000 was raised at the aerobics event.

Friday 31st October 2008.

A suspicious fire on Halloween burnt out a tipper truck and convoy truck in Howden. On their arrival, fires burning in a LDV Convoy truck and a Ford Transit Tipper were extinguished by the Fire Brigade, but not before extensive damage was caused to both vehicles. Police were keen to trace a youth who was seen near the vehicles shortly before they caught fire. On the same evening, two boys in Dedridge were mugged for the bags of sweets and nuts that they were carrying as they went 'guising'. Neither of the boys was hurt

NOVEMBER

Monday 1st November 2004.

A taxi-driver driver was robbed at knifepoint for his mobile phone and cash in a terrifying late-night attack. The attacker, who was wearing a scarf over his face, grabbed the man's neck and held a knife to his throat before demanding cash. The incident happened at about 10.40pm when the driver picked up the passenger in Uphall Station. The attacker pounced on the cabbie when they arrived at Mowbray Rise in Dedridge. The taxi driver was not injured in the attack and Police were said to be 'hunting the culprit', and were also appealing for witnesses.

Saturday 2nd November 1968.

LDC's chairman symbolically pulled the first pint at Livingston's first 'indigenous' pub, The Tower. Over the years the two-tier pub was a focal point of the community, and acquired a somewhat undeserved reputation for being a bit wild. Some great acts have performed there since it opened, including Billy Connolly and Charlie and the Bhoys, as well as a host of smaller or local acts.

Tuesday 3rd November 1987.

Livingston's economy received a huge boost with the announcement that an American electronics company, Techdyne, was to open a factory in Houston Industrial Estate, creating around 120 jobs.

Sunday 4th November 1979.

A prestigious 'show-house' in Murieston's Harburn Road was broken into by thieves, who stole absolutely everything that they could possibly carry away. Among the stolen items were a fridge, a washing machine, a three-piece-suite, carpets, bedroom furniture and a dining-room table and chairs. Tain Construction, who owned the show-home, expressed their disbelief at this unprecedented theft, and pledged to employ a night-watchman as soon as was practical. The thieves hadn't exactly been subtle – they broke in by smashing down the house's back door.

Friday 5th November 1965.

At LDC headquarters, a model of a new, state of the art shopping precinct was unveiled. It was a two-storey affair, originally with space for twenty-four retail units. Today, we know this shopping precinct as Craigshill Mall, or 'The Mall'. The Mall is today virtually unrecognisable from that first structure. In its time it has been the home of a vast array of different retail and business outlets, but today the basics are still there – Newsagent, Post Office, Chippy, Chemist and Barbers. In the past it has boasted, among other things, banks, a fishmonger, bookmakers, Clan House, a fruit and veg shop, an optician, a bike shop, a Butcher, Taxi offices and even a computer games shop. To this day, it is the hub of the district of Craigshill.

Thursday 5th November 1992.

On bonfire night, several derelict blocks of flats in 'The Streets' area of Craigshill were stripped of any wood or other combustible items by Craigshill's youths , for use as bonfire fuel. A number of adults also stole some scrap metal from the buildings. When the Fire Brigade arrived to put out the unusually large bonfires, they were showered with verbal abuse and missiles by the huge gang of youths, who even tried to face-down the police when they arrived. Amazingly, no-one was seriously injured. The flats were quickly demolished soon afterwards.

Wednesday 6th November 2002.

More than seventy jobs were created with the opening of a major new tourism information call centre in the town. Scotland's tourist board had joined forces with tourism leaders across the country to launch the £11m venture in Livingston. The national visitscotland.com complex at the Fairways Business Park was aimed at eventually handling more than a million calls a year from around the world.

Friday 7th November 1986.

Two of Livingston's outlying villages, Uphall Station and Pumpherston, received the welcome news from Scottish Gas that they were finally to get a gas-supply. The decision was largely thanks to the persistence of Robin Cook MP. There was bad news for Mid Calder and parts of East Calder though, as they were told that they would not be getting a gas supply in the near future. Parts of East Calder did already have gas at the time. Robin Cook urged patience, saying 'the more villages get a gas supply, the lesser the arguments for not giving such a supply to others'.

Monday 8th November 1999.

Managers at the Mitsubishi Electric plant in Livingston announced the imminent end of production at the plant. The news came as a redundancy response team said it had already found jobs for over half the workforce. The team, made up of local enterprise groups and other organisations, was set up when Mitsubishi announced it would close the video recorder production plant with the loss of 280 jobs. Over 140 staff had since found other jobs, while a number had transferred to the nearby Mitsubishi air conditioner manufacturing plant.

Friday 9th November 1979.

Bob Taylor aged 61 from Livingston, an LDC employee, claimed to have seen a huge UFO hovering about the ground whilst walking his dog at Dechmont Law. After a supposed altercation with the UFO, Mr. Taylor passed out for some time, possibly as long as 20 minutes. When he got home, such was his appearance that his wife believed that he been assaulted, and called the police. Other LDC employees found traces that *something* had indeed landed in the area, but no-one else saw the flying saucer. Police opened a criminal investigation for assault, to date the only police case to arise from a UFO sighting in the UK. The case remains unsolved to this day.

Tuesday 9th November 2010.

A well-attended meeting was held in Craigsfarm by angry locals upset by the possibility that Craigsfarm was to be closed and sold off, due to it apparently being 'unfit for purpose', despite having been a well-loved community facility in the town for over forty years. A strong social-media campaign was also used to save the buildings, securing their short-term future, for now anyway.

Friday 10th November 2006.

A huge JCB stolen from a building site was recovered by police, after a tip-off from an anonymous caller. It had been taken from a building site in Appleton Parkway, Livingston, when it was seen being stolen on CCTV. It was recovered in a field to the rear of Rattray Gardens, Broxburn. Anyone with further information was urged to contact Livingston Police.

Friday 11th November 1988.

Ladywell residents handed in a petition to LDC, urging them to resurface the kick-pitch near Heatherbank and Larchbank. It was used regularly by local kids, but one local mother said 'the pitch is just a mud-bath, we want the council to put an all-weather surface on it'. They were supported by their local councilor. The pitch was known locally as 'The Ashy'.

Wednesday 12th November 2003.

Council chiefs took over the management of a homeless hostel after the housing association in charge said it was struggling to cope. Bosses at Castle Rock Housing Association said its Quentin Court hostel in Dedridge was understaffed, forcing it into offering a reduced service in recent months. At full capacity, Quentin Court at the time offered 27 units of temporary accommodation for single homeless people. The partnership agreement with the council meant that the hostel would be able to offer direct access to council-run accommodation for homeless people in Livingston. Sixteen new rooms were still scheduled to be added to the facility the following year.

Saturday 13th November 1999.

An argument between three men on the footbridge between Ladywell and Howden ended with one of the men receiving a severe beating and requiring hospital treatment. The victim later claimed to have been attacked by two men armed with iron bars. Livingston Police appealed for witnesses, after what was a busy night for them following Scotland's defeat to England in a Euro 2000 play-off.

Tuesday 14th November 2006.

A young woman was attacked from behind by two youths in broad daylight as she walked through The Centre .The sixteen- year-old was approached by the boys at about 4pm.One of the youths pushed her, making her drop the bags that she was carrying. They stole her money and tried to grab her phone. The boys were described as aged between 14 and 15. The young woman was thankfully, not seriously hurt in the incident.

Wednesday 15th November 1940.

Bloom House in Livingston, originally the farmhouse building for Bloom Farm, began housing German POW's from World War Two. The prisoners were treated with respect by the locals, who even used to invite them to their local church services. Later, the POW's were moved to a new facility at Mortonhall in Edinburgh, and their place at Bloom House taken by hundreds of child evacuees from Britain's cities. Later, after forming a brass-band in captivity, the German POW's returned to Bloom House to play a special 'thank you' concert for the locals.

Wednesday 16th November 2005.

The Advertising Standards Authority publicly slammed as 'Ghoulish' a company who tried to use the murder of a child in Deans to sell their anti-truancy software to Councils and Schools. Just four days after the boy's murder, Anteon UK had sent an e-mail to 340 councils to advertise a pupil e-registration system. The Advertising Standards Authority went on to say that the move was potentially offensive and distressing to recipients. Anteon subsequently expressed 'sincere regret' over the advert.

Friday 17th November 1995.
Livingston Square, a belated attempt to give the town a conventional town centre, was opened by LDC's chairman. One of LDC's last 'hurrahs', so to speak, before it was wound up in 1996. It is located in the middle of the town, opposite the shopping centre.

Wednesday 18th November 1964.
The Lord Provost officially opened one of the town's first houses to be allocated to a so called 'overspill' family of four, originally from Maryhill, Glasgow, whose head of household worked nearby at BMC. To mark the occasion, the family was presented with a charming clock. The family actually moved back to Glasgow only a few months later.

Tuesday 19th November 2002.
BFD Group, the delicatessen supplier based in Telford Square, Livingston, went into receivership after failing to find additional funding to restructure the business. Its headquarters at Livingston's Houston Industrial Estate, and a further four sites at Warrington, Cheltenham, Derby, and London, were also to close. It supplied chilled foodservice to major supermarkets and to many independent retailers across the UK. The Livingston depot, which had a good reputation for providing steady jobs for local youth, later started again as Food Options. Many members of staff who lost their jobs after the closure were taken on by local rival 3663, at nearby Newbridge.

Tuesday 20th November 2012.
The world-famous Sky National Geographic Channel showed a UFO documentary that featured, among other things, an in-depth retrospective account of the Dechmont Hill flying-saucer incident of 1979. The program was entitled 'UFOs – The Untold Story' and has since been watched by tens of millions of people.

Friday 21st November 2008.
Three vehicles were set on fire in Dawson Avenue, Howden. A short time later, the fire service crew who had extinguished the

blazes were called to nearby Calgary Avenue, where a fire had been started in the common stair of a block of flats. The culprit was later found to have been a fifteen-year-old boy from Livingston, who was actually suspected of starting some thirty blazes in and around Livingston, including at St John's hospital and at Craigshill Fire Station. In total, the boy was thought to have caused over £100,000 of damage. Police were initially unsure if they should report him to the Fiscal or to the Children's Panel.

Thursday 22nd November 2001.

Scottish Courage, the brewing division of Scottish and Newcastle, announced a £3.5m plan to set up a new Customer Contact Centre at Deer Park, Livingston, creating over 250 jobs. It was hoped that the centre would be fully operational by the spring of 2003. The firm had already previously announced plans for a huge new distribution centre near Livingston, not far from the M8.

Friday 23rd November 2001.

ASDA in Livingston began testing new 'theft proof' trolleys in a bid to stop the disappearance of thousands of them from its car park every year. The shop, owned by U.S retail-giant Wal-Mart, had brought in the new super trolleys after more than 14,000 were stolen from supermarkets in the town during the preceding year – a staggering figure. The cost of trolley collection in Livingston had been calculated at £34,000, with ASDA having to foot more than 60% of the bill. All of its trolleys were fitted with transmitters , known as 'Cartronics', which triggered a signal if the trolley was pushed or lifted over the boundaries of the car park, locking the wheels.

Thursday 24th November 1988.

Livingston Police launched a new approach to tackling the problem of vandalism, litter dropping and the tendency of local youths to form gangs. At Knightsridge Primary School, the police, in conjunction with LDC and The Children's Panel, handed out a series of three educational comics relating to the aforementioned problems. The comics were created by Sandy Potter of Livingston Police's

Community Department. Around ten-thousand of the comics were eventually handed out to school children all over Lothian, following this initial trial.

Thursday 25th November 1982.
The two groups who were connected with the restoration of Mill Farm took the sensible decision to join forces and amalgamated. The Livingston Mill Farm Community Project joined forces with Livingston Mill Restoration Group after a meeting at Howden Park Centre. Their new name would be The Livingston Mill Farm Community Project Ltd, which it was hoped would be able to gain charitable status. A spokesman for the new group said that the past work of both groups and the future work of the new single entity would not be possible without the support of the people of Livingston, and that they intended that Mill Farm would always belong to the people and would be run by the people for the people, of Livingston.

Monday 26th November 2012.
Thieves in Livingston targeted Almondvale Stadium, but they didn't steal any money, electrical equipment or even club memorabilia. They stole a whole Porta-Cabin full of car-wash equipment. The audacious and rather ridiculous thieves simply loaded the hut onto the back of a blue flat-bed truck in the club car-park and drove off with it, in full view of some disbelieving witnesses. Baffled police were keen to speak to anyone who may have known who owned the distinctive truck used in the theft.

Thursday 27th November 1986.
A man accused of a 'drink fuelled attempt at revenge' appeared at Linlithgow Sheriff Court, where he pleaded guilty to acting in a threatening manner, making threats and causing a breach of the peace in Livingston. He was fined £200. The offence had occurred a week earlier, when the accused had got into a fight with someone in Deans and had been beaten up. He had then gotten drunk, armed himself with an air-pistol and a huge hammer, and then at midnight, went to a house in Deans to exact his revenge. He entered the house

roaring death threats, but was confronted by an ex-soldier, as he had gone to and broken into the wrong house. The drunken man tried to run but was easily caught and calmly disarmed by the soldier and another man, who then called the police.

Saturday 28th November 1987.
Former Brookside star Sheila Grier opened Livingston Children's Carnival, at The Forum. The actress also appeared in the pantomime 'Dick Whittington' at the same venue the following year. The Carnival itself was part of the town's silver anniversary celebrations, and entry cost just 50p. Attractions included mini fairground rides, animals, and of course, Santa's Grotto – as well as performances from West Lothian Youth Theatre and the local Majorettes troupe.

Sunday 29th November 1998.
A bus-load of non-local Rangers fans were attacked by locals in The Tower bar in Craigshill when they tried to enter the establishment after their 2-1 win in the League Cup Final over St Johnstone. The locals, who included local Rangers fans, did not want a cup-winning party in their pub. No-one was seriously injured.

Tuesday 30th November 2004.
Residents were threatening to turn vigilante in a bid to crack down on gang attacks and vandalism in their community. People living in Knightsridge told the Evening News that a teenage gang had been terrorising the community for several months and claimed that even community safety wardens - put on the streets to help stop crime and antisocial behaviour – were unable to control the thugs. There were several reports of wardens being attacked themselves. Shops were daubed in graffiti, windows smashed and residents had been spat at. On one occasion, a security guard at a building site at Knightsridge Primary School had to lock himself in a portable cabin because youths were hurling stones. The locals decided to take matters into their own hands in a bid to reclaim their community. They invited police and local councilors to a public meeting at the Mosswood Community Centre, which had also been targeted by the yobs. A spokesman for the group said that the area was currently

like 'Beirut' because of the gang of around thirty youths, and that if action wasn't taken by the authorities, the people of Knightsridge would deal with the yobs themselves.

DECEMBER

Thursday 1st December 1988.

Worried mothers appeared in the local paper as they handed in a petition to the council, pleading for a fence to be erected at the foot of one of Livingston's most popular sledging slopes. The slope at Dedridge's Quentin Rise was one of the steepest in the town, but there was nothing to stop children from sliding all the way down it and onto the busy road beneath it. Following several near misses involving sledgers and cars, the mothers decided to petition the council, and asked that the new fence be erected immediately, before any more snow fell.

Tuesday 2nd December 2008.
Evil serial-killer Peter Tobin was found guilty at the High Court in Dundee of the rape and murder of West Lothian schoolgirl Vicky Hamilton, some seventeen years previously. It took the jury just three hours to convict the vile predator, who showed no remorse for his wicked crime. The trial had lasted four weeks.

Wednesday 3rd December 1986.
An unemployed man from Ivanhoe Rise in Dedridge became the latest person in Livingston to have a moan about the new wheely-bin system. In a newspaper interview, he threatened to take legal action against the council and the bin-men, claiming that he would be given legal aid to do so. The man claimed that the new wheely-bin system was poor value for money for rate-payers, and moaned that the bin-men now appeared to be paid more for doing less. The Dedridge man said his little campaign had been inspired by a similar one in England by Michael Parkinson the celebrity, and he vowed that the wheely-bin system in Livingston would not last. Dedridge's councilor hit back, saying that the community council had no plans to go to court over wheely-bins, and added that this man's complaint was the only one that he had heard about.

Thursday 4th December 1986.

Fine-Fare announced that it was soon to close its giant Livingston store, and the Centre's management revealed that there were no plans for the unit to be occupied by another shop this time. Fine Fare by then had already been scaled down and really only sold food. There was some good news though, as the owners of both the Fine Fare and Woolco units confirmed that all staff from these shops would be given jobs at the new Gateway store when it opened.

Monday 5th December 1988.

Structural engineers examined the scene of a serious incident, fearing that a whole terrace of houses in the town would need to be demolished. A Livingston man was still seriously ill in Bangour Hospital, following an explosion a few days before, which ripped through his Carmondean home. The blast was so strong that it pushed the back wall of his house out a full eighteen inches, endangering the structure and causing a small fire. His neighbours were woken at 6am when the explosion occurred, nearly deafening everyone who lived in the terraced block of houses. The explosion was caused by two industrial gas cylinders that had been adapted to fit two Calor gas fires.

Saturday 6th December 1997.

Livingston appeared set for a huge American investment boost which it was hoped could create 1,800 jobs over five years. Reports that morning said a California-based research firm, Cadence Design Systems, was set to announce a project costing hundreds of millions of pounds to set up an operation at Livingston, in Kirkton Campus. This would have offered the prospect of 1800 jobs, and would be a huge boost for the town's electronics sector. A 'chill wind of uncertainty' was then blowing in the industry following the turmoil in the 'Tiger' economies of the Far East, whose electronics firms were major investors in Livingston, and in Scotland.

Sunday 7th December 1986.

The cost of some Christmas essentials in the mid 80's was illustrated beautifully by Presto's leaflets, distributed throughout the town. In addition to a generous cut-out coupon that entitled each shopper to £1 off every £10 they spent, the following festive items were on offer.

Grade A Turkey – 54p per lb
Schweppes Tonic Water 1 litre – 49p
After Eight mints – 95p
Mixed nuts in a basket - £1.99
Milk Tray Chocolates (1lb) - £2.49
Double Cream 10fl oz – 69p
Tin of premium ham (1lb) – 79p

Thursday 8th December 1994.
A double-glazing company was ordered to pay a total of £138,000 in compensation to 22 factory workers who were unfairly dismissed earlier in the year. Everest's Livingston factory workers were unfairly dismissed when the company decided to transfer part of the production to a factory in England. The sacked workers had been told at meetings at the factory on January 25th that they had to leave that very day, and that they could see management at the International Hilton Hotel in Livingston the next day about entitlement to benefits. They had been given no warning and there was no consultation about the redundancies, even though the transfer had been planned since the middle of the previous year.

Thursday 9th December 1982.
Police were scouring Livingston for a mystery marksman who fired several pot-shots at The Lanthorn's library, with what was believed to have been a high-powered, modified air-rifle. Several windows were smashed at The Lanthorn and several dead birds were found in the vicinity, with signs that they had been shot dead, though thankfully, no humans were hurt by the gunman. A local councilor said of the incident 'there is clearly some idiotic moron going about and I hope he gets caught before he wounds someone'.

Wednesday 10th December 1986.
Livingston's Community Councils publicly announced that they were joining forces to combat the town's growing dog-problem.

Several townsfolk had been attacked and huge packs of stray dogs were roaming the town. At the time, Livingston only had a dog-warden for one day each month, and it was known that irresponsible dog owners would keep their dogs at home on this day. A spokesman from Howden Community Council also highlighted the fact that several dogs had been run over on the dual-carriageway, and that this in turn would eventually lead to a serious road accident. The spokesman was also quick to point out that they were not declaring war on dogs, but rather on irresponsible or stupid people who owned dogs, adding 'there's no such thing as a bad dog, only a bad owner'.

Wednesday 11th December 2002.

Livingston Cricket Club received an award of £56,344 from the National Lottery Fund for provision of a permanent pavilion facility, comprising changing and showering facilities for players, meeting and social rooms, and food preparation and serving facilities

Wednesday 12th December 2007.

In a public statement, Livingston Police announced that they were currently investigating the theft of more than ninety Wheely-Bins over the last two months in Livingston. Across the town, dozens of private wheely bins had been stolen from outside houses, while industrial skips and large bins had also gone missing from businesses. Police and fire chiefs said the bins were mainly being stolen by gangs of youths, who then set fire to them. The Council was said to be considering suspending bin-collections in the week before Bonfire Night the following year, as around a third of the thefts had occurred at that time in 2007.

Saturday 13th December 1986.

A Livingston teenage boy was killed and his father was seriously injured following a sickening car-crash on the M8 at Harthill. There had been four passengers in the car. The family was from Deans and the mother and sister received minor injuries in the crash. Two days later, the injured father's condition at Law Hospital was described as 'progressing'.

Monday 14th December 2009.

Livingston FC recorded their record victory in a major Scottish cup tournament, demolishing Clyde 7-1 at Almondvale. The teams were level at 1-1 at half-time, but Livingston came out buzzing, with three quick goals in the first five-minutes of the second half, and the 'Bully Wee' never recovered. Livingston would face Dundee in the next round.

Tuesday 15th December 1987.

Ashraf Mahmoud, proprietor of 'Simki' in The Centre, received notification out of the blue that the rent on his shop would be increased by 100%, starting the very next week. The enraged shopkeeper, who was one of the longest serving shopkeepers in The Centre, said that in addition to now having to find an extra £16,000 per annum in rent, he also had to contend with The Centre's owners not marketing The Centre properly and with their using the same old decorations every Christmas year in year out. His biggest complaint however, was that he spent a fortune on heating his shop, only for the Centre's main doors to be constantly left open, thus letting the cold in.

Friday 16th December 1988.

Scottish actor and star of 'City Lights', Gerard Kelly, went down a storm as he performed the official opening ceremony of West Lothian Youth Theatre in Craigshill. STV star Liz Kristiansen also attended the event.

Monday 17th December 2001.

Electronics giant NEC announced that it planned to close its huge Semi-Conductor factory in Livingston, with the eventual loss of some 1,200 jobs, in what was a major blow to a local economy already reeling from the closure of the nearby Motorola plant at Bathgate. NEC, who had only recently built a huge extension to the factory, blamed a 32% fall in global demand for Semi-Conductors. The Enterprise Minister, Wendy Alexander MSP, announced a series of measures to help the unfortunate employees to re-train or find new jobs.

Wednesday 18th December 1996.

A bogus Social Worker with fake I.D tried unsuccessfully to abduct a two year-old girl from her own house in Craigshill, while her mother was present. The bogus caller, a woman, first cited false, fictitious allegations of child abuse, and then tried to convince the child's mother that she should let her daughter accompany her to receive a medical. The mother realised what was going on and made the bogus caller leave, before calling police. Police were later slated for not responding straight away, though their policy towards such incidents changed thereafter. The child was not harmed in the incident.

Monday 19th December 1988.

Halls of Broxburn announced that, as a result of their recent appearance at the International Food Exhibition in Paris, they had just been inundated with huge orders for their meat products from many countries. Meat products from the plant would soon be on their way to Ireland, The West Indies, Denmark and France in large quantities. So impressed were some of the foreign food-buyers who dealt with Halls at the Paris exhibition, that several multi-national companies from Spain and France planned to visit the plant, and were said to be interested in buying it.

Monday 20th December 1982.

LDC pulled a pre-Christmas 'cracker from their festive 'sack', unveiling plans for a new £2.5m factory which it was hoped would create 150 jobs by 1984. The factory, in Kirkton Campus, was the new manufacturing facility of American company W.L Gore Associates, and was expected to open early in the New Year. LDC's foresight in creating Scotland's first science park in Livingston, back in the 70's, paid dividends with this announcement, which came at an otherwise very bleak time for the Scottish economy, and increased the number of foreign technology companies at Kirkton Campus to five.

Thursday 21ˢᵗ December 1989.

There was a festive treat for Livingstonians at The Forum, as it played host to a packed gig – the umpteenth comeback concert by 70's rocker Gary Glitter. The singer, real name Paul Gadd, is now more famous for a string of sex offences involving children. Tickets for this Livingston gig cost from £8.50.

Thursday 22ⁿᵈ December 1988.

Lothian Health Board had a meeting and decided that the new £62m hospital in Livingston would be called St John's, after the order of knights who at one time had their headquarters in West Lothian.

Thursday 23ʳᵈ December 2004.

Scotland 'keeper Craig Gordon helped give his young cousin the Christmas present of her dreams - the chance to go out and play with her friends. The girl, aged nine, had never been able to keep up with her playmates because she had the chronic lung condition cystic fibrosis. The illness had left the schoolgirl from Livingston confined to a wheelchair, leaving her left out of many games. But family and friends, including her goalkeeper cousin, raised money to buy her an electric scooter. It meant the delighted Livingston Village Primary School pupil could now zip around with her friends.

Sunday 24ᵗʰ December 1967.

The BBC's 'Songs of Praise' broadcasted from the youth wing of Riverside Primary School, showing an ecumenical service in which several local children were Christened.

Monday 25ᵗʰ December 1995.

West Lothian's new hospital's first official 'Christmas babies' were born at St John's Hospital. Penny and Mark Bates welcomed baby Holly into the world at 12.10pm. The second baby was born that evening, the mother's waters having broken while she was carving up the Christmas Turkey at the family home in Knightsridge, at around 7pm.

Sunday 26th December 2010.

Livingston's designer outlet McArthur Glen reported record Boxing Day sales at its Livingston store, with a 38% increase in sales and a 9% increase in footfall compared to Boxing Day the previous year, in spite of dreadful weather. It was the busiest Boxing Day in The Centre's entire history. This was attributed to the marked increase of people receiving Christmas gifts of cash or vouchers as a result of the bad pre-Christmas weather, and because many canny Livingstonians were also trying to avoid the looming VAT rise.

Wednesday 27th December 1985.

A fifty-four year old Livingston man was found dead in his own home, having died from hypothermia in the cold-snap. On the same day, NEC and Motorola were advised to close due to the weather, for health and safety reasons.

Thursday 28th December 2007.

Two eleven-year-old boys and a thirteen year-old girl had to be rescued by firefighters lying on wooden boards, after they became stranded waist-deep in mud at a site near Inveralmond Community High School, Ladywell. Firefighters supported themselves on boards and dragged the three children to safety after a friend alerted them by mobile phone just after 3pm. The youngsters were taken to St John's Hospital, suffering from mild hypothermia, but were later discharged.

Friday 29th December 1995.

As the big freeze turned into the big thaw, hundreds of homes in Livingston suffered burst pipes. Festive misery was widespread as the Christmas snow and ice melted suddenly, as temperatures rose, and it was the busiest night for emergency call-outs for the town's plumbers ever recorded, and over the festive season, over 3000 such call outs were made.

Monday 30th December 1968.
An LDC housing study of Deans, Craigshill and Howden, conducted throughout the year, was concluded, regarding the structure of households within those areas. The year-end results were as follows.
Single Occupancy – 54
Couples without children – 361
Single parent with children - 30
Couples with one child – 439
Couples with two children - 435
Couples with three or more children – 351
Other – 85

Wednesday 31st December 1969.
LDC's end of year report was commented on during an afternoon radio program. It revealed some interesting facts, particularly relating to the myth that Livingston was mostly 'Glasgow Overspill' in the beginning. The breakdown of the origins of each household in Livingston then was as follows.
Livingston born – 276
Other 'New Towns' – 34
West Lothian, outwith Livingston – 527
Edinburgh – 475
Glasgow – 292
Midlothian – 221
Lanarkshire – 147
Fife – 65
Highlands – 59
Borders – 52
Essex – 41
Stirling and Clackmannanshire – 40
English Midlands – 34
Rest of Central Scotland – 96
'Other' Britain – 67
Overseas – 4

Refused to co-operate with the survey - 5

The report also revealed that 1199 households in the town had no car, 1204 households had one car, and 30 households had two cars.

Monday 31st December 2001.

Two police 'meat-wagons' and a police car descended upon The Mall in Craigshill, in an attempt to arrest a naked-man who members of the public had reported was 'on the roof of Shiel House', Almond Housing's HQ at the time. The police searched the area thoroughly but were unable to apprehend the naked man. It was later suggested that the calls had been a wind-up, instigated by drunken party-goers in Craigshill.

Craigshill High School, as seen from The Mall

Craigswood Badminton Club, late 80's.

St Andrews RC church in Craigshill

The Craigshill end of the Craigshill-Howden 'Double-Tunnels'

The iconic Cameron Iron Works

The Livingston Inn - The town's oldest pub

The old two-screen cinema at The Centre

The Skateboard Park

Try-A-Sport at Craigswood, late 80's

A young Paul Dickov when he was at Arsenal

Mark Burchill in his Celtic days

Gary Wales when he was at Hearts

Livingston after their cup-final win over Hibs at Hampden in 2004

Livingston Stories

The following pieces were contributed by ordinary Livingstonians and notable people from the area, and are written in their own narrative, either by themselves or by me after interviewing them, with two exceptions – Graeme Morrice MP wrote the excellent piece about Robin Cook, while I myself wrote the piece about Kerry McGregor, with her family's help. Some views contrast, some views concur, as you may imagine- but that's the point. Any views expressed belong to the individual contributors.

Robin Cook : Livingston's own MP
by Graeme Morrice MP

"Robin Cook represented the Livingston Constituency for 22 Years. He was first elected in 1983 when the new constituency was created following major parliamentary boundary changes across the country. He held the seat until his untimely death on 6 August 2005.

Robin was an iconic figure. His rise to the top was meteoric having served as both Foreign Secretary and Leader of the House of Commons following Labour's historic election victory in 1997.

He resigned from the Cabinet in 2003 following his opposition to the invasion of Iraq and received plaudits from people of all political persuasions for his principled stand.

Although Robin was a respected national and international figure, he was first and foremost a local constituency MP who prioritised the needs of his constituents.

Robin stood and won in six General Elections in Livingston, taking his majority from just under 5,000 in 1983 to over 11,000 in 2005. This was a demonstrable indication of Robin's popularity and the high regard in which he was held by those whom he was elected to serve.

Robert (Robin) Finlayson Cook was born on 28 February 1946 in Bellshill, Lanarkshire, the only son of Peter and Christina. He was educated at Aberdeen Grammar School and the Royal High School in Edinburgh before graduating in English Literature at Edinburgh University.

In 1971 Robin became a tutor organiser with the Workers' Educational Association. He was also elected that year as a councillor on Edinburgh Corporation and became convener of the housing committee.

On his 28th birthday in 1974, he was elected to Parliament for Edinburgh Central and held the seat for 9 years until he became the MP for Livingston.

Robin was always on the left of the Labour Party and was a member of the Tribune Group. He was an early supporter of constitutional and electoral reform although, like Tam Dalyell, he was a ferment opponent of devolution and campaigned for a No vote in the Scottish and Welsh devolution referendums in 1979. However, following the re-election of the 1983 Thatcher Government he reversed his position in favour of devolution.

He also supported unilateral nuclear disarmament and championed several liberalising social measures, including gay rights.

Robin was widely acknowledged as a brilliant Parliamentary performer and became a frontbench spokesman in 1980 and a member of the Shadow Cabinet in 1987.

When Neil Kinnock announced his intention to stand for the leader of the Labour Party in 1983, Robin was appointed as his campaign manager. Robin was also a key player in Kinnock's modernisation of the party following Kinnock's election as leader.

During Kinnock's tenure as leader, Robin served as Shadow Health Secretary, Shadow Trade Secretary and in 1994 he became Shadow Foreign Secretary, where he made his name exposing the Conservative Government over the 'Arms to Iraq' scandal following the publication of the Scott Report commissioned into the matter.

Following the death of John Smith, who succeeded Kinnock as Labour leader, Robin remained one of Labour's 'big beasts' when Tony Blair eventually took over the mantle of leadership in 1994.

Although publicly signed up to further party modernisation, Robin was never a 'true believer' when the New Labour project was born. Indeed, it was partially because of his rivalry with fellow Scot and contemporary Gordon Brown that Robin kept a foot in the left camp to demonstrate the difference between the two politically – a useful support base for any future ambitions.

Not one of the 'beautiful people' under Alistair Campbell and Peter Mandelson's image conscious New Labour, Robin had the brain to ensure his place at the top table and was rewarded with Foreign Secretary under Blair's first administration in 1997, although he would have preferred Chancellor of the Exchequer, a position that went to Gordon Brown.

As Foreign Secretary, he introduced his 'ethical' foreign policy to distinguish between the policies of the previous Conservative Government.

However, following the 2001 General Election, Robin was surprisingly replaced as Foreign Secretary – against his wishes – and became Leader of the House of Commons and responsible for reforming Parliament.

It was in 2003 that he eventually resigned from the Cabinet over the Government's support for military action against Iraq.

Robin then spent the next two years on the Backbenches until his death.

Robin first got married in 1969 to Margaret Whitmore, a consultant haematologist, and they had two sons, Peter and Christopher. Following their divorce in 1998 Robin married his mistress and former secretary, Gaynor Regan.

In his spare time, Robin liked nothing more than horse riding and horse racing and was a renowned betting pundit.

However, his greatest joy was being in his constituency, especially during the gala season and made it an absolute priority to attend as many gala day events as his Special Branch security entourage could handle!

In the last few years of his life, Robin seemed to find true happiness with Gaynor and contentment without the shackles of government. It was on one of his walking trips in the Highlands of

Scotland whilst climbing Ben Stack in Sutherland, that Robin suffered a severe a heart attack and died.

The funeral service was held on 12 August 2005 at St Giles Cathedral in Edinburgh where Gordon Brown, whom he had made up with earlier, gave the eulogy.

A later memorial service was held at St Margaret's Church in Westminster on 5 December and included a reading by Tony Blair.

In January 2007, a headstone was erected at Robin's grave in The Grange Cemetery, Edinburgh bearing the epitaph: 'I may not have succeeded in halting the war, but I did secure the right of parliament to decide on war.' The words were chosen by his widow and two sons."

Alex Stewart - Local businessman and former footballer

"I grew up in Armadale but because of my father's new job in Livingston, we moved to a new house in Craigshill in 1966, and we were the 6th family to move into the new district, to Broom Walk. My very first Craigshill memory is of viewing the 'show home' in Craigshill that had been set up. My mother later did her best to emulate its interior in our own home. I remember that until I was aged fourteen or fifteen, I thought that fresh air smelled like the special durable black Creosote paint which was once used extensively on fences in the town. I remember my first day at 'Riverside' school because it was actually held in the living-room of the headmaster, Jim Kerr, at 30 Broom Walk, and there were only three pupils. Classes were held there for the first three weeks. We then moved into the one classroom at Riverside Primary School that was completed, while the rest of the school was still a building site. Former Rangers goalie Billy Ritchie ran the first local shop which was next-door to the doctor's surgery, at that time located in a bungalow. As to the school, I remember we had a party to celebrate getting our 100th pupil. School at that time was great because new families were arriving in the fledgling district all the time, so we seemed to get a new friend every day. I was in Craigshill at the very beginning so I witnessed many changes. Craigsfarm was still a working farm when I moved there, and where the 'Parks' housing scheme is now, there was nothing, just a vast grassy slope, which was cut regularly just like Howden Park. I think at that time Howden House was still occupied, lived in, though it may have just been its caretakers who lived there. My friends and I attended a model railway club at Howden House; the main model railway was over twelve feet long. There were orchards where lower Howden now stands, and they had pears, plums and apples. I remember the adventures that I had with friends, walking what seemed like miles to pick fruit from the orchards. One of the Craigsfarm outbuildings was being used as a canteen for the construction workers who were building Craigshill, and we could always go there for a juice or a biscuit if we wanted to. When the time came to go to High School, there was no such school in Livingston so we had to get the bus to West Calder High School every day. I later did 'A' levels at Craigshill High School on a night-school course, after it opened. Then I went to Bathgate Technical College. As teenagers, we used to go to weekend discos at St Columba's, Letham, and St Paul's in Ladywell, and we also went to youth clubs in Mid and East Calder.

It was really interesting to see Craigshill grow and develop as time passed. In the early days Craigshill had a very strong community spirit, simply because people really needed other people. There were no telephones, mobiles or Facebook in those days, so as a community we were quite isolated, and that brought us together. There weren't really any buses at first and the nearest taxi company was in Bathgate, so people would help each other out with lifts and things. I remember the first taxi company, Streamline, who opened in Livingston, with three huge Austin 800's. I also remember a huge kind of 'A-Frame' sculpture that straddled the path from Craigshill to Mid Calder at one point; it had Chinese symbols on it and was supposed to be some sort of feng-shui or good luck piece. The piece had been donated to LDC as it had originally intended that area to become a park, like Howden Park is now.

At the time, LDC offered an £800 incentive to anyone who took a house in Livingston, and also offered the same incentive, or bounty, to anyone who gave up their Livingston home. At that time £800 was a lot of money, so my parents moved us to Peebles for a few years, then we moved back to Livingston, this time to Granby Avenue in Howden, pocketing £1600 in doing so. I was good at football and was signed by Hibernian when I was a teenager, it was Bob Shankly who signed me, but as well as being a football apprentice I was also an apprentice at nearby British Leyland, and learned a lot of skills from each job that I would also utilise in the other one. I later played for Arsenal, Aston Villa, Crystal Palace, Leyton Orient and Weymouth United. I enjoyed my time at Weymouth the most, because of the warm weather. I later had a brief spell at Dunfermline but then went to America to play for Detroit Express, whilst also working for America's famous General Motors; I was in the 'States for just over six years.

I have long since moved back to Livingston and become a businessman in West Lothian. Having seen the town both in its infancy and as it is today, I would say that the Livingston 'experiment' has worked, but perhaps not quite in the way that it was envisaged, and certainly not without its ups and downs. Those who wanted Livingston to work, did their best, but they were hampered by a fair few opportunists and chancers at a certain level of management within Lothian Region and LDC, particularly a certain minority element within LDC who tried to run and build the town to suit their own agenda and line their own pockets. I would also say that if it hadn't been for the socialist element in Livingston's local government and in its society, things would have been even worse for the town. Livingston was at first more like a village, even a number of villages within villages, but as the new schemes were built and the shopping centre was constructed, it became a town, as had always been intended. In some ways, Livingston in its infancy was akin to the workers' housing schemes built next to big factories in Communist States, but that didn't last long, and was only a natural stage in the town's development. A better local example of a place to compare early Livingston with is New Lanark Mill in its heyday when the town was basically run by the Mill owner, who controlled the housing, the shops and even the doctors. I do think Livingston has lost a lot of its community spirit over the years as it has expanded, but on the whole, I'd say that Livingston has changed for the better over the years. It's an established, fully-fledged town now, that is a simple fact. One really positive thing about the town that I have noticed is a lack of 'class identity', not many people bother about where other people come from in the town. There are rich, more well-to-do areas like Deer Park and Murieston, and sandwiched between them are the other schemes , which have been blighted with poverty over the years, but unlike in other towns and cities, no-one in Livingston is ashamed to tell you what area they come from. We are all Livingstonians, and it's been an exciting journey."

Brian Cullion – Making Mischief

"Oh, where do I start, Livingston, what a place. I moved to the brand spanking new Granby Avenue (120) in Howden with my parents, wee sis and brother in 1975, I was aged eight. We moved from a rather choice place in Wishaw, well a shit hole really, as my Dad had secured a job in the old PYE Transistor plant, now Mitsubishi. A great childhood ensued, but we did things I would never allow my own kids to do. My brother went under the ice in the Almond aged seven, I had to pull him out and then sneak him home, fucken' shivering, but if we got caught, my god!

Move ten years on and the friends and laughs at the famous Melville's. Best laugh was when it kicked off one night and the keystone Livi cops were running about like headless chickens as usual, every one ripping the piss out of them. One of our lads got 'felt' and was getting cuffed, while his mate was unscrewing the blue light off the squad car. The rozzers got a shout and disappeared into the night with their less than blue shiny light blazing and everyone in the taxi rank in bits, the guy was an instant hero, we played footy with the blue light until they came back looking for it. I still see those two cops and snigger. These are some of the VERY tame stories of my own Livingston."

Catweasel – A darker side to Livingston

"Catweasel lived in or near Sedgebank in Ladywell if I remember rightly. He was a scruffy old man, I think he had a family but I am not sure. Apparently he was named after a TV series in the late 70s. None of my friends or myself remember how we came to know about Catweasel, but 'chappie' was a big game back then (probably the 80s – I am 40 now and was probably 13/14 when I was playing this game) so it may have just been 'luck' when a door was found where the person inside would chase you.

Catweasel was the highlight of the night for a game of 'chappie'. We would chap his door and shout '*Catweasel, Catweasel, Catweasel*' until he came out. He would then chase you round the streets of Ladywell all night threatening to tell your parents.

One night a friend of mine chapped his door (we were all there standing behind her) and she threw an egg at him when he opened the door. The egg hit Catweasel right on his forehead and we ran and didn't stop running. I don't think he chased us that night but he shouted after us.

Looking back this man was persecuted by lots of different groups and I deeply regret being part of this horrid bit of Livingston history. Poor man, I hope he got peace and kids stopped chapping his door." Anonymous female.

"Catweasel had a dog, which we all used to throw stones at when it was in his garden. Nearly everyone 'did' Catweasel in Ladywell, shouting 'Catweasel' through his letterbox and throwing stones and mud-bombs at his house – the outside of the house was covered in marks from mud-bombs. Looking back, it was wrong". Paul, Ladywell

"I actually knew this man personally. He had children and a wife and like many people struggled to get by financially. He was a sweet person who helped people and was lovely. The children who targeted him made his life a misery and that of his son, who was also targeted.

I remember being young and crying to my granddad, who was his friend, about how people could be so cruel and how it made him so sad. Even now a long time afterwards I still feel bad for this family and the abuse that I know they suffered from people. It made and still makes me ashamed to be a human. I'm glad these people regret their behaviour and I hope they make sure their children will never act that way." Sandra, formerly of Ladywell.

Craig Smith – To Eliburn and beyond

"Growing up as a youngster in the Eliburn area of Livingston was brilliant; I cannot fault it in any way!

Moving from Glasgow at a very early age I was one of the first to move into the Eliburn area. As more and more people moved into the street from Glasgow I began to grow a very loyal group of friends from an early age, and we are still very good friends to this day, almost thirty years on, (Bollocks I am getting old!), in fact one of them was my best man at my wedding. As we grew up our parents taught us well about manners and respect etc for the older generation and property. It went for nothing as we were all wee shites at times, not extremely bad (there were a few that were though) but more mischievous! We used to make up games such as 'tarmac tig', in what we called the first park, and we played Rounders and Kerby (I may add I was awesome at that) at which we even had tournaments. We also played 'Frisbee tig' which sometimes fucking hurt, 'dripes' which was another game I was good at, 'closey '(kicking the ball in a close), 'two manny' and loads more. They were brilliant times and I know we go on and on, and our parents said the same, but kids don't do that anymore.

We constantly played football with either trees or jumpers for posts, and every Friday played against the 'Village boys. We also used to play at Peel Primary with some of the parents, which made the game more exciting and to this day we still talk about those days. We also used to play American Football in the street due to some older brothers who were into this, bloody hell I got a few sore ones trying to play that!

As I started to get a little older and puberty started kicking in we started messing about with the odd drink here and there and also smoking weed, far too much of it. The old pecker started thinking about women as well and I had the odd wee girlfriend here and there (some lasted 2 days). Starting to hit around the age fifteen mark, I started getting serious with a girl, we used to have a bit of fun, especially on a Friday as I never went to school and went to her parents house for a 'shagging' session (it normally lasted about 23 seconds, if I was lucky).

Alcohol started to be legal for me and I started drinking in pubs and clubs like Oscars/Zen etc, making a total arse of myself, which I still do to this day- but hey ho it's fun. I still work and live in Livingston and have no intention of moving out of the area either, my only wish is for Livingston to be more friendly like it used to be, it seems everyone is on edge too much, neighbours don't talk, kids aint out on the streets playing etc.

In short, growing up from an early age in Livingston was brilliant, and we still reminisce about those days."

David Cicero – Livi's pop-star

"I moved to Livingston when I was seventeen. It's changed so much since my moving from Edinburgh. I went to Melville's, which is now Club Earth, this is where I started to get inspired for doing pop/dance music. The DJ would play hi- energy music along with punk on a Sunday night. I was in a few bands and played my first gig in the Paraffin Lamp pub many moons ago, when Tom Wilson used to DJ there.

I have watched Livingston develop from a small New Town which has grown into what it is now, with all the new areas and the shopping centre, which has expanded too. The growth of it has been so rapid along with the increased number of people who live here. The bad side of this is that you need a car to get from A to B because everything is so spread out. Also, what I find a bit depressing is the amount of factories that have closed down, with losses of jobs bringing high unemployment to Livingston, and these factories are lying empty doing nothing while they are building new offices that remain 'to let' and nobody uses them, which I feel is wasting land when this could be used for better things. There are some great places in Livingston however, and this is why we decided to film my first video 'Love is Everywhere' here, which was mostly done near Howden House, which is now being developed into a new project, which is nice to see as it is not being left to rot. The development of Howden Park Centre is also great for Livingston, bringing live theatre shows and other events to the town. My video was played on most childrens' TV shows and I feel that I helped put Livingston on the map a wee bit more than what it was at the time. I also did a gig in Rainbow Records in The Centre which is now 'Gamestation'. I also came back after a successful tour to play at Crofthead Farm for a rave called The Chill, which me and my friend Ali arranged. I used to go to raves in London before Scotland was having any. Nobody knew what a rave was in those days here, but they soon did and it was a big hit. We had started something new and others followed suit and there were raves all over the place. I handed a demo tape to The Pet Shop Boys' manager when they played at the SECC in Glasgow. I then moved to London to produce my album and released my first single in 1991. The rest, as they say, is history."

David Cicero 1992

Elizabeth Ferguson –
Landlady of The Livingston Inn

"We've owned the Livingston Inn for just over six-years now, but to me the pub has a family connection to the place going back generations. In bygone days only travelers were allowed to stay at the Inn and it closed at 9pm. The poet Rabbie Burns once stayed at the Inn, and even wrote the song 'The Lass of Livingston' while he was lodged here, and even etched his name onto a window pane. Sometimes I feel like I am not just a landlady, I'm also a kind of museum creator as this is the town's oldest and most prestigious tavern, and with that comes a welcome additional degree of responsibility, which I enjoy. The Inn has changed slightly over the years, but as a listed-building, it has retained much of its original layout and structure – even the arch is still there which the coaches and horses would have passed under in days gone by. Over the years our clientele has been varied but really nice – even when we used to get the occasional streaker back when streaking was a fad. As Livingston has grown, the Inn has benefited from increased footfall, but the establishment has retained its unique charm – our regulars and the villagers like the pub the way it is so we have no plans to change it. We're still a fully operational Inn with twelve bedrooms, and there's even supposed to be a tunnel under the pub that leads to the nearby Kirk. We also appear to be haunted, as there have been a few harmless ghost sightings in the pub and in the rooms upstairs over the years. The Livingston Inn has a very friendly atmosphere and that will never change. We will always be a big part of Livingston's story."

These are the lyrics to the song that Rabbie Burns wrote while staying in Livingston. They should not be confused with a song of the same name written much later. Scotland's Bard was certainly not 'Bard' from the 'Livi Inn'. The lyrics suggest that he may have 'pulled' whilst staying in Livingston.

The bonny lass o' Livingston
Her name ye ken, her name ye ken;
And ay the welcomer ye'll be,
The farther ben, the farther ben,
And she has it written in her contract
To lie her lane, to lie her lane,
And I hae written in my contract
To claw her wame, to claw her wame.

The bonny lass o' Livingston,
She's berry brown, she's berry brown;
An' ye winna true her lovely locks,
Gae farther down, gae farther down.
She has a black and a rolling eye,
And a dimplit chin, and a dimplit chin;
And no to prie her rosy lips,
Wad be a sin, wad be a sin.

The bonny lass o' Livingston,
Cam in to me, cam in to me;
I wat wi' baith ends o' the busk,
I made me free, I made me free.
I laid her feet to my bed-stock,
Her head to the wa', her head to the wa';
And I gied her her wee coat in her teeth,
Her sark an' a', her sark an' a'.

Livingston Inn
2 Main St.
Livingston village
West Lothian
EH54 7AF

Telephone 01506 413 054
www.livingstoninn.co.uk

Joe McDermott – Coach

"My name is Joe McDermott, I worked back in the early days as a steward at Craigswood, helping with various sports and keeping the centre clean.

I also ran Craigswood Utd under 12's up to under 15's, based at the sports centre. It was great to finally have a sport centre in the town, especially in Craigshill, it was great to see all the youngsters using it and adults as well. There were a variety of sports to choose from - Karate, Judo, Gymnastics, Football, Table Tennis, Badminton, Squash and Outdoor Tennis, and of all the sports my favourite was Athletics, at which I was a qualified coach for almost twenty-five years. On a Wednesday evening we had the club night, and around eighty to 100 kids and adults would use the facility.

People came from all over West Lothian, the club is still going strong today, my boss back then was Mike McGee and the assistant manager was Alec Muir, it was a great place to work back then. I have seen lots of changes over the years, not always for the better. The price is a lot more now to use the centre as it's run like a business, it was more of a good fun exercise before then. There was one other sport I have almost forgotten, that was American Football! It was not for the squeamish may I say, and was a bit rough to say the least. The Centre has always been used for many 'Internationals' in all kinds of sport, and many famous faces have visited throughout the years. It was also a great place to meet in the earlier days in the cafeteria, where parents could watch their children doing their sports, and also see the five-a side football indoors from the large window in the café. It was a bit tasty also! The football that is! I think the centre has been a great help to the local community, especially for the children and adults alike. Saturday was a very special day for the football as the changing rooms would be packed and the parks were well used. Sometimes we had eight teams in the centre at any one time, and what a mess we had to clean if it was muddy! The centre was also used to raise vast amounts of money for various charities, which was a great thing to do, especially when you were enjoying what you were doing at the same time!

The centre was also used for visiting clubs from abroad, for example, the Livingston Athletic club would visit Olsberg in Germany and then the German club would come to Scotland every two years, and their athletes would stay with the local athletes' families, they were great times for all concerned. My old friend Tony Kemp is still with the German club, and he also was an athlete himself, here in Livingston back in the 70's and he even worked in the sport centre for a while. He met his German wife Birgit during an exchange visit with the German club and is still coaching in Olsberg to this day, he keeps in touch with me every week. I have seen lots of changes in all types of sport in general and changes at Craigswood - and not always for the better, I may add. The cost is much more now than it was back then and this will lead to the sport centre not being used to its capacity. Craigswood is much more than a sport centre- it's a place for people to meet and chat about their views and of course, do their sport. If it was not for the sport centre I would not know as many folk as I do now. For stewards who worked back in the old days of the 80's and 90s, there is a lot more packed in the centre now and it's for the good of the community and surrounding areas, long may it last for many years to come!

I think that sport has been a great thing for Livingston. Once we got the facilities, our only problem was funding. I think that there have been some periods when the cost of using the town's sporting facilities have been far too high, and at times when I was a coach, we would have to go cap-in-hand to people for grants to support our better athletes, even though they were representing Scotland or Britain at big championships! The running-track at Craigswood is surrounded by a grassy embankment, which in my opinion should have been turned into terracing or seating long ago, this would have made Craigswood not only more fan-friendly, but also more attractive to those hosting competitions, not to mention the fact that turning that embankment into a stand would have been a great economic move too. Two things that I think would be great for Livingston in future would be another sports centre like Craigswood, but perhaps at a different end of the town, and a competition-standard full size swimming pool. I think that both of these facilities would stand the town in good stead for the future."

John – A worker's reflection

"I was born and brought up in nearby Stoneyburn and served an apprenticeship with the coal-board at Whitrigg in East Whitburn. Even back then in the early 60's I could see that the government was phasing-out coal mining, so I joined the army instead as an engineer. I perhaps noticed the birth of Livingston more than some as I was stationed in the Middle-East for my six-years in the army and only came home on leave once a year, so I saw the difference in Livingston annually.

Watching Craigshill being built, the consensus among us folks in West Lothian's 'other' towns was that it was a concrete jungle in the making, and when we passed the place on buses, we would pity the poor fellows who lived or were going to have to live there, mostly because they seemed to have no facilities or amenities. As time passed the growth was maintained, but to us the new houses always looked a bit dodgy. Later, in the 1970's when I was married with one child, my family and I moved to Craigshill. The people were mostly wonderful as was the community spirit, but the houses were indeed dodgy, or at least, rubbish. They were damp, draughty and cold but this was compensated for by Craigshill's then much improved amenities. There was The Mall, two churches, two pubs, four schools and a social club. Then as Howden and Dedridge were expanded, this resulted in mass-migration to those areas from Craigshill, because those areas had better housing. This in turn resulted in Craigshill becoming more of a transient estate, but the backbone of the community was always there, for instance, when we flitted to a bigger house after our second child was born, there was no shortage of friendly people willing to help us move. There always was, however, and still are, a lot of problems with drugs and poverty in Livingston, and one can only hope that one day these problems will be rectified through care, consideration and wise investment by the government. My own working life in Livingston was limited to a few years as a fork-lift engineer, but my subsequent job saw me working at various sites in and around the town. Under various agencies, like

LDC and other public bodies, many industries were 'induced' to set up businesses in Livingston , with offers of free premises, free rates and start-up grants. Though these incoming industries were a God-send in the wake of the collapse of the mining industry, and provided much-needed jobs, they were almost all foreign-owned fly-by-night firms who would leave the town as soon as their cushy 'deal' regarding tax/premises/rates in the area expired, leaving people on the dole again, and because many were assembly-line based, the wages weren't so good for the workers and didn't give the workers many transferable skills when the companies later abandoned the town for pastures new. Many of these 'immigrant industries' were also fiercely anti trade-union and only offered limited contracts and thus, limited employment rights. This resulted in many of Livingston's workers worrying about their job security, more or less constantly.

In my own conclusion, Livingston has had its many faults, but it is still developing and has brought many benefits to West Lothian, though sadly, it has never found a sustainable alternative to mining, which was one of the main aims of the town from day one. Livingston needs more indigenous investment, from both the private and public sectors, to continue its partial success story. In this day and age we shouldn't STILL be going cap-in-hand to foreign companies, begging them to come to the town, that should only have ever been a temporary measure. Scotland and West Lothian have a great history in science and engineering, and I hope that in the future this will also be the case in Livingston once more."

Kenny Omond - On behalf of Livi Skates

"One of the things which marks out Livingston from all of the other 'New Towns' in the UK which sprang up in the sixties is the skate park.

Situated on the banks of the River Almond just across from the shopping centre, it attracted skateboarders from all over Europe for its prestigious opening in 1980 by the then chairman of the Scottish Sports Council, Peter Heatly, and it continued to attract visitors from all over the world during its heyday. Although worthy of a book in its own right, on account of the many adventures and association with most of the rich cast of personalities and characters which inhabited the adolescent Livingston, the following demonstrates the anarchic culture in which many youngsters grew up to become pro skaters, film producers, artists and other media professionals. It was the custom born out of an involvement with the Livingston Festival Gala Day held in the Howden Park for the Livi Skates to host the 'Livi Skates Pure Fun Skate Party' in the last weekend of June.

Skaters would come from all corners of the UK and further to skate the park from Friday night to Sunday evening. The floodlights installed in 1992 allowed the skating to continue throughout the night, with those requiring sustenance adjourning to the tented village of over 200 tents in the adjacent Trim Course. As well as allowing the resident aerosol artists to create amazing artwork (for which the Livi Skates won an award) round the park, music, often in the form of live bands, helped to stoke the skaters to spectacular feats of skating. The peak of the weekend was the completely lunatic 'Two minutes to Midnight' event in which skaters, often fortified by a tin or two of cheap lager, would attempt to beat the previous year's record of how many could simultaneously skate the big bowl. The sight of a snake of ten skaters carving the big bowl at high speed to the shrieks of encouragement from hundreds of skaters has to be seen to be believed. Leading up to this Two Minutes to Midnight frenzy, much skate related madness would occur fully justifying the epithet 'Pure Fun'.

This particular year the party was in full swing when a couple of officers from F Division turned up accompanied by the Environmental Health Officer from West Lothian Council, who had been 'sicced' onto us by an irate resident of Howden, who was unaware that the kids could have been in very much more harmful, chemically related, but quiet, behaviour.

Called upon to explain '*WHAT THE HELL IS GOING ON HERE?*' Kenny was elected to confess to being the organiser, if such an event could be called 'organised'. Confronting the nonplussed council officer, Kenny recited his usual mantra of the skaters being really well behaved kids who would make the Cub Scouts seem like a gang of Hell's Angels, and that they could well be involved in very much worse antisocial behaviour. Invited to come and see for himself, he arrived at the top of the half-pipe just in time to see a coffin mounted on a set of skateboard trucks and full of young skaters hurtle down the slope. To complete the scene of bedlam, flares mounted underneath the coffin belched flames and smoke as it sped down the park, finally slewing to a halt at the bottom of the 'Resi', spilling the young skaters in a heap amid shrieks of laughter and a hail of fire and smoke. There was a stunned silence as the council officer struggled to take in the diabolical spectacle unfolding before his very eyes. Giving the poor man time to convince himself that it wasn't just a bad dream, Kenny enlisted the help of the two police officers who were largely unfazed by the whole episode and knew fine well that, indeed, the kids could well be causing no end of trouble if they were not totally fixated by skateboarding. Once the initial shock had died down it turned out the council officer was a real nice guy that rode a big Harley Davidson, and played banjo in a folk group. So it was settled that the two kilowatt sound system would be turned down a notch or two and turned off after the 'Two Minutes to Midnight' spot.

Things were never the same and it really was the beginning of the end of the skate park as an independent sovereign state within the confines of the Livingston New Town. Subsequent Pure Fun Skate Parties were stuck with swingeing insurance demands which, curiously, only covered incidences of collapsing loudspeaker stands or other such calamities which might befall members of the public foolish enough to stray into what was, for a while, and agreed by skaters the world over, the most fun event they had ever had the good fortune to attend."

Kerry McGregor – The Voice

Photo Courtesy of Nicci Mackerracher

Not many people outside Lothian have heard of Pumpherston, other than when it's mentioned in the context of a certain celebrity charity football team. However, one of the Livingston area's most talented, famous and inspirational people hailed from the wee former shale-mining village on the outskirts of the town. It is impossible to tell the story of Livingston without also telling the story of some of West Lothian's outlying villages, and it is also impossible to tell the story of the people of Livingston without also mentioning Pumpherston's Kerry McGregor.

Born in 1974 into a musical family from Pumpherston, Kerry was one of Livingston and West Lothian's true stars. They say that talents 'run in the family', and with the right encouragement, that is usually the case. Kerry's grandfather, Bobby McKerracher, was a renowned and popular singer, and her mother, Margaret, is also a talented vocalist. It was no surprise then, that Kerry herself would make her own mark on the world of entertainment, and even went on to surpass the achievements of her own, talented family members.

Kerry's dad sadly died when she was just five years-old, then later, aged just thirteen, she fell out of a tree and broke her back, leaving her partially paralysed from the waist down. Kerry had been an award-winning gymnast as a child, and one could easily understand how such early tragedy and adversity in life could have crushed the confidence of most children and made them give up- but not Kerry.

Facing the additional adversity of being told that she would have to move from her own West Calder High School to attend a school for the disabled, the brave wee-girl pushed herself so hard in her rehabilitative-physiotherapy that she accomplished in just six weeks what many others would have taken a year or two to achieve, and was able, with the help of leg-braces and elbow-crutches, to prove that she could get around her existing school with a degree of competence that meant that it was safe for her to continue her education there . Not only did Kerry convince West Calder High School to let her stay there where her friends were, but a year later she experienced what she later referred to as her 'proudest moment' when she won a national 'Child of Achievement' award, after being nominated by the very school that she had fought so hard to stay at.

After leaving school, Kerry went on to study music and drama at Jewel and Esk Valley College in Midlothian, and it was at that establishment that Kerry discovered her talent and passion for entertaining. From 1993 she was in several bands that achieved chart-success, including Nexus.

Spotted by Proclaimers' manager Kenny MacDonald in 1997, Kerry then fronted the group 'Do Re Mi' as they entered The Great British Song Contest, a BBC competition whose winner would be chosen to represent the UK at the prestigious Eurovision Song Contest that year. Kerry brilliantly sang the track 'Yodel in the canyon of love' with the group, who came second in the competition to Katrina and the Waves and their song 'Love shine a light'- itself so good a track that it went on to win the Eurovision contest outright. Kerry, for her part, came out of the preliminary contest with a record deal from Polygram.

In 2006, Kerry achieved even more success, becoming a finalist on 'The X-Factor', where she was mentored by Sharon Osbourne.

She made it to week three of the live shows before being eliminated from the contest, no mean feat, especially when you consider that 2006's X-Factor is widely regarded as having been the toughest year to enter, as it was eventually won by Leona Lewis, who went on to be the most successful artist ever produced by the show.

Kerry then went on to sing at huge events in Blackpool, and then performed in front of millions of people on the Saturday night National Lottery draw show. She toured with Jay Brown in 2008 and sang with a famous Tenor at the Edinburgh Fringe in 2010.

Kerry, of course, was an actress as well as a singer, and appeared in numerous stage, TV and radio productions during her career, including the BAFTA award-winning 'The book group' on Channel 4, and also in the BBC's iconic kids' TV show 'Grange Hill'.

She always found time to help other people, and when not singing or acting, committed a lot of her time to helping charities that assisted children, the disabled, and women. She even helped to launch a new brand of designer clothing for women who use wheelchairs, and appeared on GMTV when the range was launched. Kerry even wrote for the Spinal Injuries Association and Diana Memorial Fund, and was involved with the BBC's 'Beyond Boundaries'.

In 2010, aged just thirty-six, Kerry was diagnosed with Bladder Cancer and had to undergo a prolonged serious of treatments, but at first, even that didn't get in the way and she courageously carried on with her charity work. She received a standing ovation from the crowd at her last performance in 2011, at a pre-Paralympic event held in Newcastle. Her last project was to have been a charity duet with another West Lothian star, Susan Boyle, but sadly Kerry and Susan weren't able to complete the project.

Kerry tragically lost her brave battle with Cancer in January of 2012, and nearly 500 people attended her funeral. Upon news of her death, tributes poured in from fans all over the world.

Of her disability, Kerry once said "My life changed completely for me from an early age. I had been very involved in singing, ballet and drama. In some people's eyes it could be a hindrance but in my eyes it's not. If anything, it gives me all the more reason to kick my heels in and go on. I am determined and I will achieve"

Kerry certainly did achieve. We saw her stunning beauty, her magical smile and her awesome talent, not her disability. Livingston and its directly outlying villages haven't produced many other famous people in recent years, save for a certain Cicero, a few half-decent footballers and a minor author or two, but Kerry McGregor stands out as one of the truly great people to have come from the area. She wowed us with her voice, she dazzled us with her beauty, and she inspired many of us with her sheer determination. Livingston, West Lothian, Scotland and indeed the world will never forget her. There is a tribute-page to Kerry on the internet, where you can learn much more about her, its URL is

www.kerrymcgregoronline.com

The Night of the Big Blaze – Keith Tait

"In the early days of Livingston, my wife, myself and two young children stayed in Leven Walk, in one of what I believe they called the Jespersen flats, which were built a bit like a life- size Lego set – slotted together. Our number 73 has since been demolished – but I have many memories of our times there.

I remember standing in the kitchen on a sunny summer's evening (shows how long ago that was!). I had the window open and was leaning on the sill, when I became aware that it was possible to move the whole wall panel a good six inches in either direction. A sort of early patio window, I suppose.

Then there was the time our upstairs neighbours, two 'sonsie quines', left their bath running. We got all the water directly through into our living room, there being nothing but concrete slabs between us and their bathroom. I thought it was raining at first, but hot water? We weren't living in the tropics -but I digress. The true excitement came on the night of the great rubbish store fire. This was in the days before wheelie bins. All rubbish went into the rubbish store, inside the flats. As we were on the ground floor, we were right next to it. Quite ripe on a sunny day, I assure you.

Anyway, our top upstairs neighbour was a sales rep. He used to abandon piles of free samples in the rubbish store. Once I went in and the place was stacked full of phones - complete with batteries- and they were right next to a pile of half filled paint tins- he'd obviously been decorating. Well, the rubbish men were coming next day, so I decided just to leave it to them. Bad decision.

Later that evening we were watching a programme about the Holocaust on the TV when I was sure I could smell smoke. Then there came an almighty banging on the front door.

When I opened it, the whole hall was filled with rancid reek. Flames were shooting out of the rubbish store, blistering the paint on our door. There stood the upstairs neighbours. They didn't need to tell us to get moving. Then the stair lighting melted and all the lights went out.

We gathered up the kids and ran for it, out the opposite door and onto the grass. With a flashing of blue lights and screaming sirens, the fire brigade pulled up. We all ran round the corner to watch the fun.

Once they got the hoses connected, they had the blaze out in no time. They simply poured gallons of water in through the remains of the window. True professionals. I spoke to one of them and he said it happened regularly, kids set the stores on fire for a joke. But batteries and paint tins don't mix, do they? We never found out the true cause of the conflagration, but we lived with the smell of burning rubbish for weeks. The LDC put in new stair lighting, and the store was totally rebuilt, but even with redecoration, you could never quite get that odour out of the close. Ah memories..."

The McDermotts. A family made in Livingston

The McDermott family from Livingston are, to all intents and purposes, a family that was truly made in Livingston. Davie, 37, and Jenny, 35, grew up in Ladywell and Craigshill respectively. Their own and their family's development are typical of that of many families and individuals in the town. In many ways, they are the very type of family that the people who conceived the town in the early days envisaged to become its local populace.

Davie went to St Mary's Academy in Bathgate, while Jenny went to Craigshill High and Inveralmond. The couple met in the mid 1990's at Livingston's only nightclub, moved in together to a council flat in Ladywell in the late 90's, had their first child, Marc, in 2000 and their second child, Kerry, in 2003. They moved to Craigshill in

2002 as they needed a bigger house and wanted to buy instead of renting from the council. Both of them have worked at various factories and warehouses in the town since leaving school, Davie now works in warehousing, while Jenny works in social care. Davie also helps to run a kids football club in Craigshill that has teams for various age groups which compete against other local sides, and also train regularly. Here are some of their thoughts on life in Livingston.

Davie- "I think that one of the best things about where I live is the fact that there is still a good community spirit, a lot of the town is made up of soul-less schemes full of new builds where people hardly know their neighbours – Craigshill isn't like that at all. I come home from work each day and see Jenny and my kids, the kids aren't 'dumped' with a nanny as some other couples may choose to do. When I was a boy and a young teen we saw ourselves as being from Ladywell first, Livingston second. The town seemed more like a collection of villages rather than a single town, but that changed as I grew up, chiefly because I played a lot of football, which meant that I knew people from every district and visited them whenever I wanted.

I wouldn't exactly say the rivalry that once existed between districts in Livingston was outright 'gang warfare', though sometimes it could get a bit dodgy. Playing football with guys from the other districts helped to break down those barriers, as did things like working with and partying with people from other districts as we got older. I grew up in Ladywell but moved to Craigshill, where I'm now a 'Craigshill man' as some of my friends say, though I have slightly different memories from some of my friends, as I didn't grow up in Craigshill, but that's never been an issue and my family and I love it here. I think the sell-off of council housing in the 80's was bad for Livingston, as it now means that extended families are often dotted all over the town rather than living in the same scheme, but that's happened everywhere, not just in Livingston. I'm lucky in a sense, as my parents and my sister now live in Craigshill too, as does Jenny's brother and his family. I think Livingston is an okay place to bring up a family, there are worse places that's for sure – but I have noticed a distinct lack of community spirit in certain areas of the town, particularly the more expensive/exclusive areas where people live in little enclaves. I think the sports and leisure facilities for families in Livingston are reasonably good, but expensive, and I think that the local schools are excellent. In contrast to other places in Scotland, less families here choose where to live on the basis of what school's catchment area they will be in – unlike in places like Glasgow or Edinburgh where people often have to stay in unsuitable housing just to ensure that their kids get into the 'right' school. To help families, I'd like to see more long-term jobs being created in Livingston, and more childcare options to help more parents to work, but that's a central-government issue, not just a Livingston one, and I suppose it's all about money at the end of the day. I do think that it's sad that you don't see as many children playing outside as you used to. Adults today seem to have less toleration for children playing outside, which is a shame, as that, along with going to school, is how kids learn their social skills. Whether it's video games and DVDs keeping them indoors, or their parents fear of them getting hurt, who can say? My kids go out to play without being asked to as long as the weather's OK, it's second nature to them. I don't think I want my children to live in Livingston when they grow up, much as I like the place, I want them to see the world first. All in all, I think Livingston has been an adequate place to raise a family, but I fear for job prospects for people in the town in the future. I lived in London for a while when I was younger, and I wouldn't want to bring my kids up anywhere near such a place, Livingston will do nicely for us."

Jenny – "I think there should be a university in Livingston by now, and maybe a technical college as the range of courses offered at West Lothian College seems too limited and focused solely on preparing students for specific jobs in Livingston, jobs that might not be here in ten years. In general I think Livingston is a good place to bring up a family, particularly because most of the streets are cul-de-sacs and there are good footpaths, bridges and underpasses – that's one thing about Livingston that I think many people might take for granted. Compared to a city, Livingston is safer and easier for kids and families to walk about with less chance of being run-over. I would like to see more effort from the council put into things like after-school clubs, sports and music for kids. My single favourite thing to do in Livingston is to go on long walks in its parks during the summer, with my family and my friends and their kids. Almondell is our favourite place."

Marc, aged thirteen, who attends St Margaret's Academy – "I like Livingston because it's small, and there are plenty of places to play football for us. I would like there to be a different football club in Livingston because Livingston FC are rubbish and have hardly any fans. The only thing I don't really like about Livingston is that the adults smoke and drink too much, and there are too many drunks staggering about the streets. My fave thing to do in Livi is to play football."

Kerry aged ten, who attends St Andrews Primary School in Howden- "I think we need more places for us to play in Livingston that aren't as far away from our house. I really like the people in Livingston, there are lots of them and they're very nice. My most favourite thing to do in Livingston is when we go on bike-rides with friends and family up to Bangour, and you don't even have to cross one road!"

Stuart Pearson –
An Edinburgh man in Livi

"I moved from Edinburgh to Livingston seven months ago. To be honest I have struggled to cope with the culture shock. I find Livingston lacks atmosphere, transport could be a lot better as could the footpaths. If you're going places on foot, for example to Ladywell Park & Ride, you can find yourself walking on a lot of muck and grass verges. My best memory of this town would be a football match between Livingston and Hibernian, although it's the coldest game I've ever been to. I went home happy though, as Hibs won 2-0!"

A rap about Livingston – By local Livi hip-hop star 'Tyme Lord', AKA Sean O'Donnell, aged 21

Tyme Lord

"Rumours true or false are equally appealing,
Pain comes in variety, but you need to make me feel it
How am I supposed to survive with a meal like this?
All people go out of their way to make you feel like shit,
It's hard to tell apart the difference between laughter and guilt,
That's why all relationships expire faster than milk,
Relapsing smack addicts, delve back into bad habits ,
The buildings are cracked, damaged and no one's stabbing to kill
It's that place that I hate but the home that I love,
I've grown such a custom to coping with nothing,
I'm prone to disgust and destructive assumptions,
So showing love is something I'm not putting up with,

Cards close to the chest, you might think change is in the hands of tight fists,
I don't know how to cope, life's already far too complicated,
I've always been frightened to light spliffs in Knightsridge,
Never mind the polis, it's the young teams trying to confiscate it,
The mind is complex but I'm astoundingly literal,
You're the crowd of the typical, I'm surrounded by imbeciles,
No one can keep a secret, we confide in deceptive honesty,
They say that visitors from space are hidden in the Dechmont forestry,
I'm not a fan of accusations ,I'll try it before I knock it ,
'Cause the lighter I just bought is in one of my friends pockets,
Just like the women Livi ain't a pretty sight,
I'm getting too dizzy on the Witch hunt for Lizzie Bryce,
Actors describe their attraction to lights,
Spent most of my time sitting, I only see the office lit,
I'm casting my line, it's like you're casted for lines,
I'm trying to make a living and you're fishing for a compliment?
Another fresh slate? I'm done with hammer and chisel, Mannerisms horribly planned decisions, I've had it with being asked to listen,
It's hard to imagine how it is here, I can't create a vision,
why is the word 'live' in Livingston, when I can't make a living?"

You can find Tyme Lord's music on the website Soundcloud, under the username seanodonnell-1

Alec Muir – Sport in Livingston

"I worked at Craigswood Sports Centre from the very day that it first opened in 1980 until 2004. I then left to work at the smaller centre at East Calder and am now based at head-office in Bathgate, running the football- pitch side of things for West Lothian. I sometimes wonder where all those years have gone; so much has changed for sport in Livingston during those years. In the twenty-four years that I worked at Craigswood the structure of the place changed and evolved greatly, in some ways mirroring the changes and evolution of Livingston itself as a whole. When we first opened we had a sports-hall, a Hi-Tech Room, two Squash courts, and upstairs there were pool tables and an indoor bowling mat. Later we put a weights-gym upstairs, but today the upper level of the building contains a boardroom and a dance studio, the latter of which hosts all kinds of dance and fitness classes. The main entrance to the sports-centre used to have a large revolving door, but that's long gone now. In the end, it was nothing but hassle as parents with pushchairs struggled to get through it and kids were always picking up minor injuries because of it, so we got rid of it. Where today there is a state of the art gym, there used to be a cafeteria area and a general purpose room. The cafeteria area was where users and spectators met before and after their sports sessions, and the 'GP' room was used for Judo, Boxing and Table-Tennis, though it was sometimes hired out for children's parties too. As the years went by we acquired full-sized football pitches, both to the east and to the west of the centre, and in the mid 80's we installed a running track, and later a pavilion for the athletes who used it. One of the biggest events of the 80's at Craigswood was when our running track was used for 'Sport Aid', which was part of the wider movement to relieve the famine in Ethiopia, runners were encouraged to 'run the world' and get sponsored to do so.

We are actually at this time just beginning a nine-month project to make an even bigger, better, 130 station gym in a newly built extension on the centre's west side, which partly covers the old changing rooms for five-a-sides, which have been demolished. These are currently exciting times at Craigswood, a bit muddled because of the move, but on track to become an even better facility.

Where once out the back we had ash-surfaced tennis courts and hockey pitches, we now have four '3G' football pitches, which are extremely popular.

When Craigswood first opened it was the only centre of its type in West Lothian, but thankfully there are now also facilities at Linlithgow, Bathgate, East Calder and Broxburn. In the early days, one of the few drawbacks about Craigswood was its location, as unless you lived within walking distance or had access to a car, the centre was difficult to get to via public transport, there wasn't even a bus-stop for the district of Craigswood for many years, but there is now.

One of the best aspects of working at Craigswood and in sport in West Lothian has been seeing people come in to the centres as youngsters for 'Try a Sport', then a few years later they would come in to use the facilities as adults, and later with their own kids, even their grandchildren sometimes! We have been very pro-active in encouraging that trend over the years and we really do offer something for all of the family. Craigswood Sports Centre has been of great benefit to the surrounding community too, there's no doubt about that, and I feel proud and privileged to have been a part of that. The building at Craigswood is owned by the council, but it is run by a leisure trust. Of course we have had issues in the past regarding funding, but that happens everywhere.

Craigswood isn't Livingston's only success story when it comes to sports facilities either. Look at Excite Leisure Pool, formerly Bubbles, that has been an overwhelming success for the town. When it first opened, some people lamented the fact that it doesn't actually have a competition size swimming-pool, just for swimming lengths in, but that hasn't mattered, it has flourished and its footfall has increased every year. I would like to see a competition size 'proper' swimming pool in Livingston one day though, I think it would be great for the town, though there is still one nearby at Bathgate. I also think that a town the size of Livingston and its surrounding area needs an ice-rink, we haven't had one since Icelandia closed. More generally, I also think that the town would benefit greatly if it had a new multi-purpose conference and exhibition centre, like the much-missed Forum, where big sports events, gigs and exhibitions could be held. Livingston's location and travel links would make it an ideal location for something like that. Not a lot of people know this, but the SFA considered relocating Hampden to Livingston in the early 90's, yes, they really were going to build the new national stadium in Livingston! It wasn't to be though, and Hampden was partially refurbished instead. Livingston's great travel links were the big factor in its favour when that decision was made, but ultimately, that alone wasn't enough to convince the SFA to relocate.

All in all, I think sport has been of immense importance to Livingston as it has developed, and I'm sure that will always be the case. There are exciting times ahead. Sport in Livingston can't just stand still, it has to keep evolving, just as the town itself does, and both will continue to do so. We have great facilities, great staff and great customers. I'm just delighted to have been a part of it all over the last thirty-three years."

Bette– Go West

"My family moved to the town from Edinburgh in 1976 to the oldest part of the town, Craigshill, where we lived for thirty years, quite happily!

There was no Centre then, just the Mall, the hub of the community. There was an air of optimism and togetherness, everyone came from somewhere else, lots of young families, good local schools, doctors, dentist, library, youth wings, all within walking distance, with no roads to cross. There were playgrounds and play schemes so it was an ideal place to raise a family 'living in the country'. The buses left a lot to be desired, but we managed. The centre came in stages, eventually, now there is no real need to travel to Glasgow or Edinburgh as we used to do for shopping.

The Development Corporation were innovative with housing and the landscaping was wonderful, they had good funding to encourage jobs and people to the town, and along with funding from the European Social Fund, urban aid did a really fair job of shaping the town.

Many organisations existed, reflecting the era. Drop-in centres for mums with babies and children (most had no extended family around) and the local churches were instrumental in bringing people together and piloting Good Neighbour Networks town-wide.

Our consciousness of the past remakes us, but as our eyes dart here and there at what Livingston shows us, different years and decades buried make their impact and our hearts are built up by them one on top of another. So we will not only understand and enjoy our town more with this book in our hands, we may also find it easier to understand ourselves."

O'Driscoll - Coming to Livingston and doing youth work - From Honest Toun to New-Town

"I first moved to Livingston from Musselburgh in 1988. Moving in with my girlfriend who was an original Craigshillian that had arrived there in 1966 when she was just two weeks old. I'm happy to say we are now married with kids. Anyway, I digress. It wasn't long before I came to realise that this place was not like The Honest Toun, Musselburgh being a smaller place I knew most folk and took my happy go lucky personality to Craigshill, where my nods, smiles and hellos were at best met with surprise and sometimes with outright hostility.

I decided to go out and explore the nightlife, and with four locals in tow we went out for my first visit to the Tower Bar (upstairs). The whole time, I felt people were staring at me and I was very uneasy. This was confirmed when a guy with a huge Mohican followed me to the loo and stared at me as I urinated. I returned to my table and asked my pals 'Is it safe for me to be here?' I expected someone to say something like 'aye that's ma brother over there' or some other reassuring phrase, but they turned round in unison and said 'No!', so we then left the bar. My second visit to The Tower was with my girlfriend's wee brother and his pals, they had a football team called The Rowdies and they were all underage at the time. We were sitting in merriment having a right laugh when they all went silent and started whispering. The source of this was a guy who had just entered the pub.

'Shhhh! It's the local radge' they said.

'Who the f**k is the local radge?' I asked, still laughing. The name they called him by sounded like a Viz character. They pointed to a wee skinny guy at the door and I was unimpressed till they told me about some of his exploits with slabs, hammers etc. I had moved into somewhere mental!

In 1992 I started my first part time youth work post in Riverside Youth Wing. It was a baptism of fire but the beginning of a career that I have pursued to this day. I worked with the Community Education Worker and a group of kids who had mostly been through the youth justice system following an incident with a stash of petrol bombs. I still remember many of their names - Ping, Rab, Dawson, Johnny, Brian (a gifted graffiti artist), Humie and Jason to name a few, there was also a kid who had a missing finger which he had accidentally sawn off. On one of the first nights we allowed them to use the video camera (worth about 2 grand then) they went into Edinburgh with it, filmed themselves hanging on to the bonnet of the car as it swayed on the road, shouting 'Big tits' at women and simulating solvent abuse. Ian thought they'd nick it and he'd lose his job. Another evening, Johnny, who had been messed up through involvement in a cult, turned up with a big hunting knife. I demanded he give it to me and he refused. I kept demanding and he kept refusing, the louder I got, the more defiant he became, eventually he left the building. Ian was shocked when I related the conversation and reliably informed me that Johnny would have as soon given me it in the guts. Jason, the one who had the car, died in it a few months later (RIP). Strangely enough most club nights were good nights and the banter was brilliant.

Having got the bug for youth work I started working in different clubs and my next one was Carmondean drop in at Nether Dechmont. The kids I worked with there were not as hardcore but they had their own issues. My first group were a bunch of stoners who would come into the Drop-In to listen to Teenage Fanclub and eat the food I prepared, they were the most laid back bunch I have ever worked with, just as I was getting used to them and getting somewhere on our regular discussions about drugs, a new, younger group appeared, more full on and challenging. They were culturally different too, mainly into rap and 'gangsta' culture and the sounds changed from Indie to Cypress Hill and Ice T. Among the younger group there was one big gangly challenging boy, he shouted, bawled, bragged and presented new hassles every week. One week he wasn't there and I asked the kids where he was. They couldn't stop laughing till they eventually told me he was in a secure unit having 'shagged a dug' as the kids put it. I bumped into him in later life and could not get that particular image out of my head. Often my issues in Carmondean centred around stealing, there was one group of three 'creepers' who would burgle houses when occupants were in. We did work to explain how and why that was wrong. Another group tried to steal my car. They were good times in the Drop-In.

In the 90's I also worked in Mosswood, Knightsridge. Again, it was not for the faint hearted - then as now there were issues with alcoholism in the scheme. One lad who was in his early 20's and enjoyed a drink, went by the name of Beveridge, the irony was not lost on me. By then this was around 94/95. There were many and varied challenges - one notorious family used to lend the kids money then get heavy with them, I was threatened several times for not allowing them access to the building. There was also a kid who suffered severely from epilepsy and was banned from the building because he had tried to burn the place down. Every week he would ask to get in and every week it would be explained that there would be no club if he had his way. The other kids would then sneak him in, only to end up shouting for assistance as he fitted on the floor. Mosswood was the most challenging club as the kids were all members of the 'K-toi' and that bond was stronger at that time, than any other in their world. There was one lad who consistently overstepped the mark in the abuse he gave workers, he was 19 and already a parent, he once threatened to get a hit carried out on me, I told him that gangsters don't go to youth clubs.

In 1995/6 I started working in the related field of community development but not in Livingston. In 2003 I returned to youth work in the town but not as a youth worker, but as a community worker in the youth team, managing youth workers and youth clubs. I was based in a high school and met the kids at break and lunch times. Again the work was beset with characters, like the kid from Knightsridge who had a carpet fetish and would hang around outside the carpet shop and run in and sniff the rugs and carpets when security weren't watching. A group of kids from the school went on a trip with me to Dynamic Earth, at the souvenir shop they were thieving the gifts, when I challenged them and told them to stop, they replied 'okay dad, we'll stop!' I was cringing with embarrassment.

There was also the time the Jannies picked up something like a rubber band in the corridor only to find it coming to life, it was a snake. One of my best memories was of a volley of abuse I got from a kid in the corridor. I found out his name and he shared it with the kid who threatened a hit on me in Mosswood, it was his son.

After the school my remit widened and covered almost the whole of Livingston, the whole area and a couple of villages to boot. A few years back we opened Riverside Drop In again on Mondays ,right back where I had started. The kids are different now but still have many challenges. Many of them are gay or bisexual. I have had to give gay girls a row for sexually harassing my female staff and once when I confiscated a bottle of MD20/20 from a tall camp kid called Jordan, he retorted 'Put it in the fridge for me.' The work has changed too, it is more issue based. In Forestbank, Ladywell, we did a poverty exhibition, the kids wrote the narratives in characters but they were definitely first- hand accounts. We also do work with the Fire Service whereby kids go to the fire station for a week instead of school (usually kids with issues). Some go to the Phoenix Programme- a sort of cadet force. One such kid learned too much and set fire to the learning pavilion at the fire station. When he was caught the CCTV was checked in relation to fires in the Livingston area, and he had been responsible for thousands and thousands of pounds worth of damage.

Despite all the stories I have given they are not a fair representation of youth work, for every one of these tales there are ten stories (not as exciting) about successful and developmental youth work. I should also say though that all the young people I have worked with have provided colour to my life and I am grateful for the time with them. Many of those referred to have gone on to do well in life and are good parents and contributors to their communities."

Eddie Anderson – Livingston's Journalist

"Being chief reporter of the Livingston Post and Editor of the Herald & Post was the best time of my working life.

It gave me a unique insight into the lives of the people of the then New Town.

It wasn't all good news, of course, with all life in there, including murder, rapes, fatal fires and assaults.

But that's comparable with any town of a similar size and they're not the stories that remain most embedded in my memory.

Where Livingston excelled was in the pioneering spirit of its early inhabitants.

One of my best memories of the Livingston Post was turning up at almost every event that was held in the town. Nothing was too big - whether it was the fight to keep Craigshill High School open - or too small - such as a bring-and-buy sale in aid of one of the many local organisations that were springing up on almost a daily basis. And the Livingston Festival, played out at Howden Park, merited its own special pull out. It was the social highlight of the year for many of the town's inhabitants - and one where age was no barrier to enjoyment.

Sadly, it was spoiled by Political Correctness, one of my biggest pet hates, when the committee was infiltrated by people who thought that parachuting into the park, adding assault courses and marching the Military was not the way to go.

They felt we should all be pacifists and, sadly, the event petered out, robbing the townsfolk of their big day. It was also one of the few events that brought everyone together, whether they were from Craigshill, Deans, Dedridge, Knightsridge or Ladywell. Fortunately, there are now moves afoot to resurrect the festival.

Sometimes small events had big impacts. At the time when homeless people were being lodged in bed and breakfast establishments, there was a sudden rise in 'doss house' accommodation. Plans for one such 'doss house' establishment were lodged at Ladywell by the then Windmill Lodge, later to become known as Da Vinci's and later D-Luxe. The inhabitants of the Barratt homes at Eliburn were up in arms at the proposal, but due to the fact that the Windmill Lodge had a public house licence, it was easily converted to a hotel and so one of the town's most popular watering holes was born.

And talking of the Barratt Homes, who can forget the sight of Jason Donovan and Kylie Minogue when they were in the town? If only we knew then what we know now. I remember interviewing Brian Orr, sadly no longer with us, the man responsible for bringing two of the world's biggest names to Livingston. He told me he had been sitting watching an early episode of 'Neighbours', and had an inkling that it might just take off. He took a note of the contact details at the end of the credits, phoned the program makers and offered to become their UK manager.

Brian's was typical of the spirit that personified the early Livingston dwellers.

The Livi Post was a 'must read' paper, where gossip could be authenticated and rumour established.

Rumour was always rife in a new town, where varying backgrounds came together in a clash of cultures. And never more so that when Union Carbide applied for planning permission for a plant in Livingston after more than 2,000 people died in their premises in Bhopal, India. Until that point, Livingston Development Corporation (LDC) had been mainly faceless in the town. That was all to change with a backlash against the proposals that forced LDC into a heated public meeting at Deans, where townsfolk left LDC officials and board members in no doubt about the depth of their feelings. The corporation was forced into retreat and townsfolk had found their collective voice.

Although there was always a clamour for LDC Board meetings to be opened to the public, there wasn't a stampede to Sidlaw House (later to become West Lothian House and now the site of Primark) for the Friday monthly meetings. But some of the most momentous decisions affecting the town and its people were made in the small boardroom. One was the decision to object to proposals for a mega-centre on the site of the former British Leyland at Bathgate. Under the stewardship of its chief executive, Jim Pollock, LDC had a direction of travel, albeit it was not always obvious to local residents. One such plan was that Livingston would always be the sub-regional shopping centre of the Lothians, second only in importance to Edinburgh. The Bathgate proposals threatened to stop Livingston's retail development in its tracks. Had it gone ahead, there would have been no Debenhams or Marks and Spencer in Livingston, only a half-built and probably half empty shopping centre as the Livingston legacy.

Now Livingston centre is a thriving, bustling array of shops and shoppers. But remember the shopping centre 'trolley gangs' that dominated the pages of the Livi Post for weeks. As soon as you arrived at your car, you were 'pounced' upon by half a dozen people, eager to take your trolley back for the 20p 'reward'. OAPs trying to augment their pension were soon muscled out by the aggressive gangs, who dared you not to let them take your trolley back. Soon, some of them were making up to £30 a day, many of them also signing on at the same time.

Upping the deposit to £1 soon rid the town of their menace, as shoppers were eager to reclaim it for themselves.

The opening of Melville's, later to become Zen and then Club Earth, saw Scotland's first custom-built discotheque located on the banks of the River Almond. How many revellers remember attempting the Trim Track on their way home, not always a good idea as it turned out. While Colin Jackson was making a name for himself at the Craigshill Social Club, Bob Reid was packing in the punters at Melville's. And if you didn't fancy dancing the night away, you could always take in a meal at the riverside restaurant, now the Island Bar at Club Earth.

While Livingston was making a name for itself as a go-ahead town, with plans to bring in a professional football club, Knightsridge seemed to be heading in the opposite direction. I remember a meeting with one of the local police chiefs when he said that the district in the north of the town was fast becoming a 'no-go area'. At the same time, a protection racket was taking hold in the area, and one of my most memorable interviews was at 4.30am, when I had a tearful meeting with a local shopkeeper, who feared for her life and felt she would probably be murdered at her job. The world's ugliest CCTV was installed in the district, a sure sign to outsiders of the problems. Thankfully, residents took matters into their own hands and were determined to rid the area of its unwanted and, on the whole, unwarranted reputation. The unemployment centre was a great help, providing activities for idle hands, as well as a meeting place. The demolition of parts of Knightsridge, which had been built as a Scottish Office experiment in high-density living, eased much of the problem. Names were changed to protect the innocent, with Malcolm Way becoming Moncreiff Way, and today the district enjoys a settled existence with The Vennie and Mosswood Community Centre both thriving local centres.

Craigshill is still commonly known as 'Crazyhill' but today it's more a term of endearment and is often used more by residents of the district than by outsiders. The resurgence of the Craigshill Gala Day has helped foster the community spirit that caused LDC a headache when residents refused to leave Craigshill when the original flat-roofed Jespersen flats were refurbished. Board members thought there would be a stampede to take up offers of re-housing in the newer district of Dedridge. But most of the people forced to move out of Craigshill on a temporary basis were quick to return to their refurbished homes and today the district is probably the most settled of all in the town. Dedridge, on the other hand, now has a more transient population than most, with the inherent problems that brings.

197

Working and living in the town could sometimes bring the odd awkward moment, such as when covering the courts, then bumping into the accused in the local shop, hostelry or community centre. Discretion was always the better part of valour and people soon came to know that their secrets were safe with me.

It was a sad day when the Livi Post finally folded, but it was really an incremental closure, moving out of the old Centre (across from the Paraffin Lamp) into Lammermuir House. From there it moved to Bonnyrigg before one day morphing into the new free newspaper, the West Lothian Advertiser. That guise was short lived, giving way to the Herald and Post, which soon gained affection amongst the populace, mainly for its campaigning and crusading ways, plus a tendency not to take itself too seriously.

It had always been an ambition of mine to become a newspaper editor and I will be eternally grateful to the people at the Herald and Post for giving me that opportunity. Work became a place I couldn't wait to get into and the laughs the job provided will live with me forever. Of course, it wasn't without some dangers. I remember going to interview someone in a block of flats at Craigshill. While everyone round about him was being decanted, he defiantly refused to leave his home. It sounded like a great story, but the alarm bells soon started ringing when he locked the door firmly behind me on my arrival. Then when he turned his music up as loud as it could go when I was making my best efforts to interview him, I realised something was amiss. And then it dawned - no-one knew where I was. Fortunately, I was able to eventually make my escape. But being taken 'hostage' was a lesson learned and to this day, I never go anywhere without letting it be known where I am heading. And remember, that was the day before mobile phones.

One of my happiest encounters was being woken up at 5.30am, or to be more accurate, my wife was woken up at 5.30am. I remember hearing her say "yes that's him". When I got to the phone, I could tell it was the voice of an elderly man. "Is that Mr Anderson from the Herald & Post?" he asked. "It sure is," I responded in my best 'I'm not really asleep' voice. "I wonder if you could help me," he added, "My cat is stuck up a tree." This was a Wednesday morning and when I asked him how long it had been up there, his reply was "since

Saturday." Startled, I asked him why he was only phoning me now and was equally startled by his reply: "I didn't know your number or where you lived, and have been phoning all the Andersons in the book since Sunday."

As it turned out, his cat was higher up a tree than any cat I have ever seen, but we did manage to reunite the elderly gentleman with his pet, thanks to the paper's Countryside Ranger, who wrote a regular column. When I asked the gentleman why he had phoned me, I was delighted when he said "because you seem like the kind of paper that would help."

And that, I hope, summed up my stewardship of the Herald & Post. We were a paper that would come out and help you. Every week, at the same time as we were looking to break the biggest stories in the district, we were also fathoming out ways in which we could help out a local charity or deserving cause.

Sadly, the Herald and Post, like the Livingston Post, is no longer with us.

But one legacy lives on - and to this day is still helping raise money for local charities. That's the Miss West Lothian event, set to celebrate its 20th anniversary in 2014. Its origin was an attempt to create our own local celebrity. Over the years, I have been involved in helping to raise more than £100,000 for local charities and good causes. One of the most memorable periods was when the Herald & Post took over the running of the West Lothian Toy Appeal, now administered by River Kids. We moved it into a different league, bringing The Centre on board - with the money from the Christmas displays going to the appeal - and involving lots of local companies in collecting toys for local kids at Christmas.

Life was a lot of laughs, whether it was Drew doing his dazzling mindreading demonstrations, or Amber and Stuart giving their unique look at life. But being chief reporter of the Livingston Post and Editor of the Herald & Post was a real privilege and I wouldn't change a minute.

Sure there were sad times, and always that panic after the presses were printing that you had probably made some momentous error, but it has provided me with a thousand and more memories and a unique opportunity to share in the growth of a town that I have come to love.

The Livi Post and the Herald & Post may have come and gone. But had they never been there in the first place, Livingston would have been all the poorer for it.

And of that, I am absolutely certain . . ."

Susan Docherty - Livingston - My Memories

"Livingston is my hometown and I have so many good memories of the place that no matter where else I choose to settle, home is still Livingston. Mum and Dad were relocated here as part of the Edinburgh (Dad) and Glasgow (Mum) overspill that populated the town during the 1960's. Born in November 1979 at Bangour Village Hospital, I was raised in Craigshill (or 'Crazyhill' as some lovingly called it) for the first six years of my life and lived latterly in Carmondean before leaving to go to University in Glasgow at aged seventeen.

I attended Letham Primary School and it was here that I received a good, solid foundation to my academic studies. The school was led by a very firm but fair Head-Teacher in Ms Rutherford and I absolutely loved it! Lots of friends, great teachers and a wide choice of after school activities were contributory factors to my fond memories of my primary years. And it is still the only place that served the famous 'Sausage and Bean Pie' which I have never tasted ever again since!

More specific memories are the Thursday Club at Letham Primary on a Thursday, Miss Tennant's Recorder class, Scottish Country Dancing at school with Miss Tennant and Mrs. Davidson, and our fabulous school plays like 'Joseph and the Amazing Technicolour Dreamcoat'.

I started Craigshill High School at aged eleven and was only there for one year until its closure in 1992. Whilst the building was becoming run down, the school had a lot going for it. Some may argue that there was a falling school roll but the class sizes were more manageable and the teaching standards at the school were higher than I experienced in the school that I was subsequently moved to. We tried to save our school in the only way we knew how, and that involved staging protests and barricading ourselves in the gym hall. Some may call it rose-tinted spectacles but it is with hindsight that I realise the extent to which the closure was detrimental to staff, students and to Craigshill as a community. Livingston had a long tradition of gala-days. Each district of the town at some point had their own gala-day. I always took part in my local gala-day in Craigshill whether it was being a flower girl to the Gala Queen, Miss Lucina Fazakerley, in 1990, or taking part in the sports competitions between the local primary schools. Those days were special and they really did bring people together from the community. Unfortunately, I don't think it's the same now. The gala-days need to be restored to their former glory.

I found a hobby at the age of five when a neighbour took me along to a majorette class in a local primary school. I remember the class teacher saying that I had picked up three different twirling tricks in my first night and from then, I had caught the twirling bug! My neighbour continued to take me to the class for about a year but then I moved house and could no longer go.

Many years later, a classmate told me about a new baton twirling class at Riverside Primary, so I talked my mum into letting me join at aged eleven. It was the Riverside Twirlettes, run by a fabulous lady called May McLaughlin and coached by her equally fabulous daughter, Angie, and between them they turned a small local club into a great success. Many of the girls that started at Riverside went on to twirl for Scotland in national and international competition. The club regularly graced the local newspapers with stories of winning accolades, and were also involved in the filming of the 'Make it in Livingston' television advert, promoting the town. The Riverside Twirlettes are part of the great sporting history in Livingston and I am extremely proud to have been a part of it."

Anonymous –Choose Livingston

"Choose Life. Choose Livingston. Choose camping up 'Dechie. Choose a brilliant 'Tarzie. Choose The Mall. Choose that bloody shopping centre that seems to have grown in size each time you visit. Choose Melville's/Zen/Earth on a Thursday night then suffering at your work on the Friday. Choose Bottle Erchie. Choose Da Vinci's, Grand Central then Club Earth 'cos there's nowhere else to go. Choose getting chased away from Craigshill Chippy when you were wee and not from Craigshill. Choose the Mouse n Cheese in Ladywell. Choose swimming doon The Almond. Choose Mad Rab at The Ferns. Choose wondering what the Trim Course is for. Choose fighting over taxis at 3am even though you only live five minutes' walk away. Choose teenage battles against every other district in the town. Choose the Livi-Punks and the Paninari. Choose The Rowdies. Choose getting a job in a foreign factory only to be paid-off a few years later when it moves to somewhere cheaper. Choose not having a fucking scooby who Lizzie Bryce was. Choose a game of 'Kerby'. Choose the old two-screen cinema. Choose pitch n putt oot yer nut on a Saturday morning. Choose seeing moving to Eliburn as moving up in the world. Choose The Workshop. Choose vandalism. Choose The Lanthorn Sheep. Choose vowing never to return to the town's nightclub, then going back the next week. Choose a job in Sky. Choose having to explain where Livingston is to folk from outside Lothian. Choose telling the same folk that the town isn't named after that bloody explorer. Choose Nothing to Say. Choose Cicero. Choose being able to drive at any time of day without hitting gridlock. Choose roundabouts. Choose a bloody good hospital. Choose Jim Devine. Choose Scotland's first Technology Park. Choose your local pub. Choose low crime-rates. Choose safe paths for your kids to get to school. Choose one of Britain's most innovative towns. Choose your future. Choose Livingston."

Primary Sources:

The Good People of Livingston
Scalacronica – Sir Thomas Grey
Archives of West Lothian Council/LDC
West Lothian Courier Archive
The Livingston Post Archive
The Scotsman Archive
The Herald Archive
BBC Archives

Bibliography:
The History of Livingston – William F. Hendrie
Livingston Lives – Emma Peattie
Livingston : The Making of a Scottish New Town – Elspeth Wills
Scottish Battlefields – Chris Brown PhD
Cromwell and Scotland – R Scott Spurlock
Dynasty : The Stuarts – John Macleod

Ian Colquhoun Biography

Ian was born, brought up and educated in Livingston. He was a warehouseman until a violent incident in Ireland in 2002 that saw him almost killed in an unprovoked arson attack. He received 65% burns and lost his legs and the fingers on his right hand, spending seven weeks in a coma. After a year in hospital, during which he underwent twenty operations, Ian learned to walk again with prosthetic legs. He studied history at The University of Edinburgh from 2004, and released his first book 'Burnt' in 2007. He has since released several books and also works as an actor and stunt-man. He has appeared in Downton Abbey, The King's Speech, Ocean of Fear, River City, Taggart, Casualty and Sunshine on Leith.

He also does a lot of work for various charities and works as a concert promoter and musical/singing talent-scout. His other books are:

'Burnt – Beaten, burnt and left for dead. One man's inspiring story of his survival after losing his legs.'

'Drummossie Moor –The Irish Brigade and the Battle of Culloden.'

'GarryOwen! - The Seventh Cavalry and the Battle of the Little-Bighorn.'

'Over the hills and far away – The ordinary soldier.'

'Nine Lives – A Self-Help Book for Amputees.'

'Jihad! – Battle for the Sudan.'

'Edinburgh – On this Day'

www.iancolquhoun.org.uk

Printed in Great Britain
by Amazon

56157288R00122